PEIRCE MILL

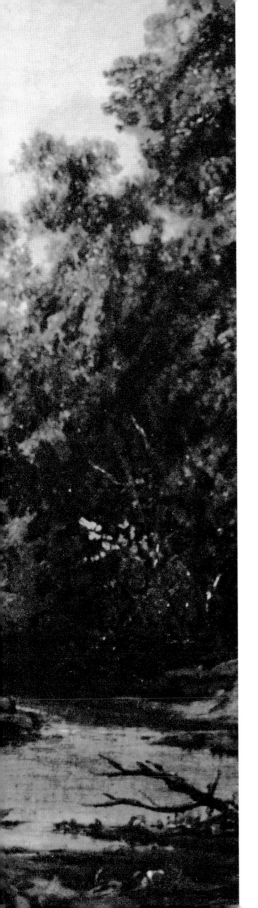

PEIRCE MILL

Two Hundred Years
in the Nation's Capital

Steve Dryden

ERGAMOT

Washington, D.C., and Berkeley

BERGAMOT

www.bergamotbooks.net

Editor in Chief Gail Dickersin Spilsbury
Designed by Denise Arnot

Distributed by: Friends of Peirce Mill
www.peircemill-friends.org

ISBN 10: 0-9760905-5-4
ISBN−13: 978-0-9760905-5-7

Front cover: Peirce Mill, ca. 1830, artist unknown.
Courtesy Theodore R. Hazen Jr.

Inside back cover and flaps: Panorama from
Pierce's Heights, by Alexander H. Clements, 1848.
Courtesy Albert Small.

Printed in China by Oceanic Graphic Printing

To JILL

Contents

Acknowledgments

The great mill wheel, its last revolutions accomplished, lay idle on its oaken shaft bedecked with dried mattings of greenish pond weed and grass, motionless now, the deep-throated steady grumble and roar as much a memory as those other diurnal sounds, far more faint yet persistent, that had echoed in all weathers season after season from dawn to dusk. —William Styron

WHEN I JOINED THE FRIENDS OF PEIRCE MILL more than ten years ago, I had no substantial knowledge of the history of Washington, D.C., "beyond the monuments." That expression is shorthand for the places that define the capital as a community with stories of its own— stories mostly unrelated to the noisy federal government and its transient politicos. As I became more familiar with the mill's two hundred years on Rock Creek, I was struck by how little was really known about the Peirce family and the National Park Service's stewardship role. It was obvious the mill needed a comprehensive history, and I am grateful to the Friends' board for agreeing to sponsor this project. As suggested by the Styron passage above, from *The Confessions of Nat Turner,* the sight and sounds of the mill are deeply embedded in our collective unconscious, and the memory deserves far greater cultural recognition.

Many people assisted me in research and writing. Special thanks are due to: Mary Belcher, a kindred soul devoted to unearthing the untold stories of Washington, and whose handsome art and historical insights enliven this book; Mike Dolan, for aid beyond the call of duty as he read and edited a complete draft of the manuscript and made many helpful suggestions; Ted Hazen, miller-millwright extraordinaire and inexhaustible source of Peirce Mill information; and Robert Sutton, chief historian of the National Park Service, for generous assistance in obtaining a nineteenth-century Peirce collection. Richard Abbott, Philip Gaudette, Don Hawkins, and Bob Kapsch were very helpful in reading and critiquing the manuscript.

At the National Archives, Robert Ellis provided indispensible assistance as I made my way through the labyrinth of District of Columbia records. George Briscoe also patiently answered my questions and helped locate important files.

I am also grateful to: Anne Alexander, Eddie Becker, Jack Blodgett, Ellen McCallister Clark, Beth Corrigan, Bill and Tom Cammack, Darren "GoDadde" Gailen, Ida Jones, Megan Leining, Bob Lundegard, Dolores Milmoe, Simone Monteleone Moffett, Wes Pippenger, Mary Rice, Paul Smith, Sue Swisher, and Perry Wheelock.

Staff members at the following institutions were very helpful: the Chester County, Pennsylvania, Historical Museum, the D.C. Archives, the Hagley Museum and Library, the Kiplinger Library, and the National Park Service's Museum Resource Center.

Italy-based Gail Spilsbury, a fervent fan of Rock Creek Park, put her Bergamot Books imprint behind this project and served as a wise and attentive editor. It has been a pleasure to work with her, even at great distance. Denise Arnot created the book's beautiful design.

For grants and financial support, the Friends of Peirce Mill thank: the Association of the Oldest Inhabitants of D.C., the National Trust for Historic Preservation through the Dorothea de Schweinitz Preservation Fund for Washington, D.C., the Humanities Council of Washington, D.C., the National Park Service Historic Preservation Fund administered by the D.C. Historic Preservation Office, the late Lummy Hagner, and Albert H. Small.

Finally, I wish to thank my wife, Jill Eden, for providing generous technical support and love. She is the blessing who makes it all possible.

Steve Dryden
Bethesda, Maryland
September 2008

Note: This book's spelling of Peirce follows the version used by most Peirce family members, and the current spelling of the name. Pierce Shoemaker (1816–1891) sometimes spelled his name with an "ie," as did his son, Louis Pierce Shoemaker (1856–1916). This latter spelling was used by the National Park Service and others until the 1990s, and direct quotations in the book from that period use that spelling.

Foreword

STEVE DRYDEN'S BOOK ON THE PEIRCES brings to life a fascinating family history from the early years of Washington, D.C. Landowners and farmers, millwrights and mill owners, flour merchants, brandy makers, horticulturists, civic activists, developers, philanthropists—the Peirces, and their Shoemaker, Cloud, and Carbery cousins, were involved in much of the daily life of the nation's capital from the time of its creation through the early twentieth century.

This volume also traces the National Park Service's stewardship of the mill, which began in the 1930s. I have worked closely with the Park Service since 1988, when I became a volunteer miller's helper at Peirce Mill. At that time, the mill operated on weekends, and occasionally during the week, grinding both wheat and corn. My job was to bag the products—unbleached white or whole wheat flour and cornmeal or grits—and sell it to the public in two- and five-pound bags. We had loyal customers, people who preferred naturally stone-ground products as an alternative to what is produced on steel rollers and enriched to replace nutrients lost in processing. Our visitors loved the mill experience: the meshing of wooden gears, the smell of freshly ground flour, and the sound of falling water.

The Friends of Peirce Mill board, *left to right,* Tom Blackburn, Philip Gaudette, Adam Sieminski, David Lyman, Richard Abbott, Steve Dryden, Sheila Ploger, and Ken Faulstich. *Photograph by Adam Sieminski, 2008.*

One day in April 1993, miller Ted Hazen and I heard a loud thumping from the gears, which signaled trouble. I was told to shut off water to the wheel and the mill ground slowly to a halt. It turned out that rot had severely damaged the main shaft, and the attached "pit gear" had moved out of position and no longer engaged the gears that turned the millstones. That made further operation of Peirce Mill impossible.

My initial hope was that the Park Service would find the necessary money to repair the mill. After three years, it became clear that this perennially underfunded federal agency had no hope of an appropriation for this work in the foreseeable future. At that point, I felt that somebody needed to act before the deterioration already taking place had gone so far that it would be too late—or impractical—to restore the structure and the milling machinery. Thinking that there would be support in the community from our "friends," who knew the old structure and regretted its closure, I wrote a letter to the *Washington Post* in September 1996, which resulted in the creation of the Friends of Peirce Mill (FOPM), a nonprofit group to raise money for the restoration.

Steve Dryden was one of those who joined as we launched FOPM. When the first board convened, he was elected vice president and I president. We have retained those positions ever since, though some of the others on our eight-person board have changed over the years.   Currently, in addition to Steve and myself, our board includes Sheila Ploger, Philip Gaudette, David Lyman, Tom Blackburn, Ken Faulstich, and Adam Sieminski.   Previous board members who made major contributions included Gene Hines, Phyllis Myers, Paul Smith, Bob Day, and the late Philip Ogilvie.

Left, preservation craftsman Steve Ortado works on repairs to the mill's internal structure. *Center,* restoration specialists Gus Kiorpes and *right,* John O'Rourke at Peirce Mill. *Photographs by Richard Abbott, 2008.*

The fish ladder at the Peirce Mill dam. Completed in 2007, the passageway allows herring, alewives, and other migratory fishes to swim upstream in Rock Creek to spawning areas. The century-old dam, unrelated to the operation of the mill, was built to provide a scenic waterfall for visitors to the area. *Photograph by Steve Dryden, 2008.*

After incorporation, FOPM's first task was to size up just how big a project we were taking on. With some of our early grants, we hired a well-regarded English millwright, Derek Ogden (fortunately living nearby in Virginia), to survey the condition of the milling machinery and tell us what it would take to get it back to running condition. We then retained architect Baird Smith (of Quinn Evans Architects) to survey the condition of the building. We contracted with Robert Silman Associates to do a detailed engineering analysis of the structure. Kirk Mettam of Silman led that effort.

We were surprised to learn that extensive repairs would be needed, including a complete renewal of the internal supporting structure for the floors, repair and strengthening of the heavy timber framework holding the milling machinery, and removal of unserviceable wooden gears and shafts. For the actual restoration work, we have relied heavily on historic preservation contractor Steve Ortado for repairs to the internal structure of the building, and on mill restoration specialists John O'Rourke and Gus Kiorpes for the repair and replacement of the wooden milling machinery. Architect Ward Bucher and his team prepared a plan for a recirculating water system to power the waterwheel.

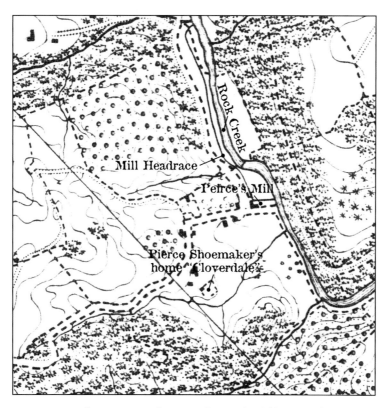

This 1861 map shows a Peirce plantation fruit orchard (designated by a block of small circles) near the mill. Partial restoration of the orchard could expand the historical integrity and educational potential of the mill complex. Albert Boschke map. *Courtesy Library of Congress Geography and Maps Division.*

Repairs and construction began in 2002, and continued steadily over the next six years. A new waterwheel shaft was installed in June 2008. New and repaired milling machinery parts, a new waterwheel, and the system supplying water to the wheel are to be installed next. Our hope is that by mid-2010 the gears of the mill will be turning and that visitors will once again enjoy the sights and sounds of a nineteenth-century water mill in the heart of the District of Columbia. This achievement will represent a fitting footnote to the Peirce Mill history so ably presented in Steve Dryden's book.

Richard Abbott
President, Friends of Peirce Mill
Washington, D.C.
September, 2008

In Appreciation—Restoration of Peirce Mill

ALL OF THE INDIVIDUALS AND COMPANIES named in the foreword are to be applauded for their fine work—sometimes at less than their full fees—on this public-spirited project. The initial cost estimates for the mill restoration have grown over time, and as of September 2008 approach $1.5 million. Fortunately, FOPM had considerable success in raising money from foundations, several of which gave us multiple grants over the years. One of our early members, the late Mrs. Randall H. "Lummy" Hagner Jr., was key to our fund-raising success, through her extensive contacts in the local philanthropic community. Lummy felt a personal connection through her ancestor and Peirce neighbor, John Adlum, and we regret she did not see the restored mill.

Organizations that made major contributions to the project included: the Kiplinger Foundation, the Marpat Foundation, and the 1772 Foundation. Local businesses that supported the project included the Clark Construction Company, PEPCO, Chevy Chase Bank, Fannie Mae, and Deutsche Bank. The National Society of Colonial Dames of America in the District of Columbia organized a well-attended fund-raising event. Artist Barbara McNear contributed a handsome sketch of the mill that we used on FOPM note cards. On the initiative of D.C. Councilmember Mary M. Cheh, the District of Columbia government made a very generous contribution. (A full list of our donors can be found by visiting: www.peircemill-friends.org.)

We are grateful for the support of our principal counterparts on the Rock Creek Park staff: Superintendent Adrienne Applewhaite-Coleman and Assistant Superintendent Cynthia Cox. We could not have fulfilled our goals without their continued cooperation and goodwill. Other Rock Creek Park staff who helped us over the years included: Benny Goodman, Kari Grabinski, Laura Illige, Dwight Madison, Anne O'Neill, Julia Washburn, Perry Wheelock, Maggie Zadorozny, Simone Monteleone-Moffett, and Meghan Hagerty. At the National Park Service Regional Office we welcomed the support and encouragement of Regional Director Terry Carlstrom, and Joe Lawler, Darwina Neal, and Rebecca Stevens.

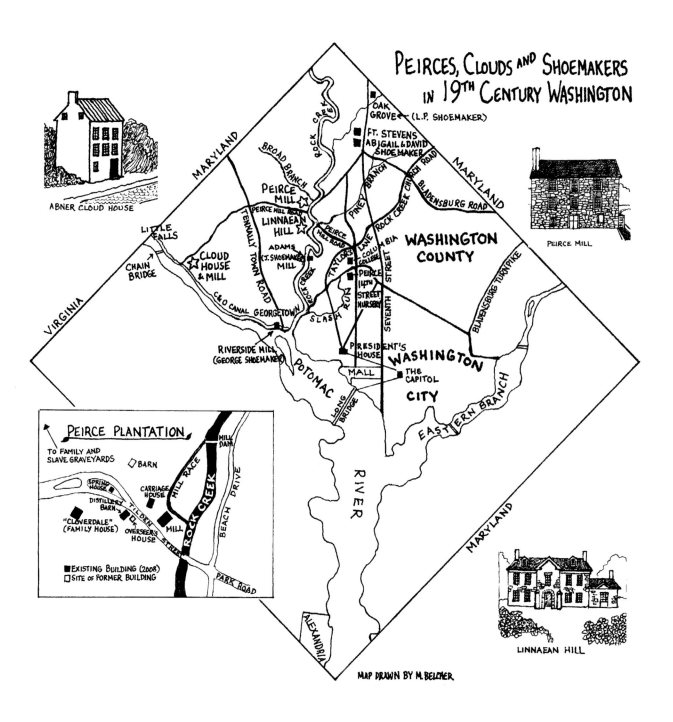

PEIRCES, CLOUDS AND SHOEMAKERS IN 19TH CENTURY WASHINGTON

ABNER CLOUD HOUSE

PEIRCE MILL

LINNAEAN HILL

OAK GROVE (L.P. SHOEMAKER)

FT. STEVENS

ABIGAIL & DAVID SHOEMAKER

MARYLAND

ROCK CREEK

BROAD BRANCH

PEIRCE MILL

PEIRCE MILL ROAD

LINNAEAN HILL

ADAMS (J. SHOEMAKER) MILL

LITTLE FALLS

CHAIN BRIDGE

CLOUD HOUSE & MILL

TENNALLY TOWN ROAD

VIRGINIA

C&O CANAL GEORGETOWN

ROCK CREEK

SLASH RUN

TAYLORS LANE

PEIRCE

COLUMBIA COLLEGE

PINEY BRANCH

ROCK CREEK CHURCH ROAD

BLADENSBURG ROAD

WASHINGTON COUNTY

SEVENTH STREET

BLADENSBURG TURNPIKE

PEIRCE 14TH STREET NURSERY

RIVERSIDE MILL (GEORGE SHOEMAKER)

PRESIDENT'S HOUSE

WASHINGTON CITY

MALL

THE CAPITOL

POTOMAC

LONG BRIDGE

RIVER

EASTERN BRANCH

MARYLAND

MARYLAND

ALEXANDRIA

PEIRCE PLANTATION

TO FAMILY AND SLAVE GRAVEYARDS

BARN

MILL DAM

SPRING HOUSE

CARRIAGE HOUSE

DISTILLERY BARN

"CLOVERDALE" (FAMILY HOUSE)

OVERSEERS HOUSE

MILL RACE

ROCK CREEK

BEACH DRIVE

TILDEN STREET

MILL

PARK ROAD

■ EXISTING BUILDING (2008)
□ SITE OF FORMER BUILDING

LINNAEAN HILL

MAP DRAWN BY M. BELCHER

1

"Many Fast Flowing Streams"

FOR GEORGE WASHINGTON, the ten-square-mile, diamond-shaped piece of land at the fall line of the Potomac River was an ideal location for the nation's capital. Choosing the site provoked heated debate among American leaders, hinging on the issue of slavery and other national problems, but one of Washington's arguments involved simple geographic observation. The area had "many fine clear-water springs at ground level suitable for drinking" and "many fast flowing streams to power griste mills . . . ," he wrote.[1] One of those swift streams was Rock Creek, which ran north to south, bisecting the territory.

Beyond two port settlements, the area was sparsely inhabited. The Piscataway Indians, who once hunted the surrounding forests and fished in the creek and river, had been pushed out more than a century earlier. The decision in 1791 to select a Potomac setting for what would become Washington, D.C., opened up new opportunities for young entrepreneurs involved in milling.

Tobacco, the cash export crop of Maryland and Virginia, dominated commerce in the ports of Georgetown and Alexandria, located on opposite sides of the river at the farthest point inland on the Potomac before the Little Falls blocked navigation. Shrewd Scottish merchants controlled the tobacco trade, and also had a strong hand in the importation of manufactured goods. But tobacco had become a losing proposition. "Decay was everywhere in Tidewater Potomac as the eighteenth century ended," Frederick Gutheim commented in his classic history of the Potomac region, referring to the exhausted soils and ruined estates of the tobacco lands.[2]

Meanwhile, trade in flour, milled from grain grown in the uplands of the mid-Atlantic region, was on the rise. Even before the American Revolution of 1775 to 1783, demand for exported American flour was growing in Europe, the Caribbean, and South America. After the disruptions caused by the war, would-be mill builders began to trickle into the Washington area.

Georgetown and Federal City, or City of Washington, by George Beck, 1801. This
view from the west includes the Rock Creek bridge, located between the two
settlements. *Courtesy Library of Congress Prints and Photographs Division.*

In the two decades following the revolution, three men of Pennsylvania Quaker heritage—Abner Cloud Jr., Jonathan Shoemaker, and Isaac Peirce—established mill operations after settling near the confluence of the Potomac and Rock Creek. Little had changed in the technology of milling since the days of the Roman Empire. Conduits channeled water to turn a wheel with cups, providing the energy to drive a grinding stone. It was exhausting and often dangerous work, but every village or town had to have a way to grind wheat and other grains, if not with waterpower then using animals, wind, or bare hands applied to mortar and pestle.

Abner Cloud, son of a mill owner and farmer of English descent, was about forty-one years old in 1801, the year he completed a house for his family on a mill site just to the west of Georgetown, later to be bordered by the Chesapeake and Ohio Canal. Jonathan Shoemaker, whose ancestors were German, was a versatile and ambitious man who already had been a manager of the Pennsylvania Hospital in Philadelphia, a delegate to the state's constitutional convention, and a justice of the peace. In January 1804, Shoemaker bought forty-two acres of land and an existing mill on the east bank of Rock Creek, near what is now the National Zoo. Well connected with the Virginians among the new country's leadership, the forty-eight-year-old Shoemaker soon would send his son, Isaac, to operate Thomas Jefferson's Shadwell mill outside Charlottesville.[3]

Isaac Peirce, born in 1756, had grown up in Chester County, Pennsylvania, where his father's land adjoined that of Abner Cloud's family. He married Abner's sister Elizabeth. By the mid-1790s, Isaac and Elizabeth had seven children. Isaac belonged to the fourth generation of immigrant Peirces, whose ancestral home was in Somerset County in southwest England, and his family already was experienced in the mill business. First arriving in the Washington area in the mid-1780s, Isaac apparently worked with the Cloud family for several years. In 1794, he acquired 160 acres and an existing mill on Rock Creek, a mile north of the mill that Shoemaker would buy about a decade later. Isaac paid 750 British pounds for the well-developed property*, which included a dwelling house with brick chimney, barn, slave quarters, and more than 750 apple and other fruit trees.[4] The 320-square-foot wooden mill structure stood at the north end of the narrow track named "Gift" that began at the mouth of Rock Creek at Georgetown.

To better understand these three Pennsylvanians, it helps to recall a few facts about the unique Quaker tradition, and about the traditions of the milling trade in which the men worked. The Society of Friends (the formal name for the Quakers), an offshoot of the sixteenth-century English Puritan movement, emphasized the individual nature of Christian belief, and saw

* Though the dollar was declared the U.S. currency unit two years earlier, pounds were still in circulation.

no need for ordained ministers and consecrated buildings. Though morally strict and plain in dress ("Away with your skimming-dish hats, and your unnecessary buttons on the top of your sleeves," admonished sect founder George Fox), the Friends did not believe, as did some Protestant groups, in monastic isolation or withdrawal into remote communities. Friends "looked upon the material world of daily toil and daily bread as God's world in which men were called to do His will," observed Frederick B. Tolles in his groundbreaking work on Philadelphia's Quaker community, *Meeting House and Counting House.*[5]

Despite their industriousness, the Quakers endured fierce persecution by the British authorities, both for their stubborn refusal to swear an oath of loyalty to the crown, and probably for the competition they presented to established business. Members of the breakaway Christian group had moved in great numbers to the Pennsylvania colony founded in 1681 by Quaker William Penn, son of an acclaimed British admiral. Penn put his own view of the material world this way: "True Godliness don't turn Men out of the World, but enables them to live better in it, and excites their Endeavours to mend it."

Quakers prospered in part because of their reputation for honesty and dependability. As millers or mill owners, these characteristics were particularly important, because ever since medieval times, the milling craft had been viewed with suspicion. Brown or yellow grains easily could be and often were adulterated by unscrupulous millers with sawdust or other filler. According to rumor, mills had hidden compartments or chutes, cracks in the floor, or other devious ways to siphon off flour for the miller (the miller was to take only a set toll in flour for his services). One of the *Canterbury Tales* portrays a classic example of the meretricious miller, whom Chaucer calls a bully and a thief. Even if he were honest, the miller performed so basic and essential a service—and traditionally was so secretive about his craft—that envy and ill will inevitably arose.

Since Quakers would not serve in the military, they could devote themselves exclusively to whatever business they chose, and the practice of intermarriage among Quaker families allowed a pooling of financial resources and a degree of cooperation unavailable to many other merchants and farmers. On the eve of the American Revolution, Chester County, the home of the Clouds and Peirces, with a Quaker population of about 40 percent, was economically well off and politically stable.[6] Prosperity, and in some instances conspicuous wealth, were hallmarks of the entire Quaker world, both in the Americas and in Britain. In keeping with this culture of upward striving, Abner Cloud, Jonathan Shoemaker, and Isaac Peirce planned to profit by *owning* a mill, not actually operating it. They would leave that sweaty work to a miller.

The Quakers' economic success tempted numerous adherents to abandon the movement's moral rigor and move into the mainstream of the emerging American society. Although in the 1750s, the Philadelphia Friends opted for a return to orthodoxy, the breakup of what was called the "Holy Experiment" in Pennsylvania was, in the view of most scholars of Quaker history, inevitable.[7] Personal morality, or public piety, was not only at issue, but also the greatest political question of the day: should Quaker men, brought up on a doctrine of strict pacifism, fight in the French and Indian conflict, and later, the Revolutionary War? For the Clouds and the Peirces, the issue became unavoidable in the fall of 1775, when the Pennsylvania Assembly ordered universal military service for all adult males. Quaker "meetings"—the organizational unit of the Friends—required not only that members flout that order, but also that they refuse to vote, pay taxes, or hold office in the evolving revolutionary government.

Two years later, in September 1777, the war came to Chester County, when a force of 15,000 British soldiers marched through the East Marlborough township, home of the Peirces and Clouds, to confront General George Washington's troops in the Battle of the Brandywine. Losing that engagement to General William Howe, the British commander-in-chief in America, Washington withdrew toward Philadelphia, leaving Chester County undefended. For months, the British plundered the area, even molesting Quaker communities, despite the Friends' neutrality or, in some case, outright sympathy to royal rule.

The Clouds were among the families whose property was damaged by the British. Whether this pushed Abner Cloud Sr. into the Chester County militia is unclear, for Crown forces may have targeted him for his pro-Revolutionary activities. In either case, by May 1778, Cloud, along with several Quaker relatives, had joined the military unit.[8] An "Isaac Peirce," presumably the same man who would move to Washington in the 1780s, also is listed in the same company of the Eighth Battalion of the militia. At some point during those early years of the Revolution, Abner Cloud Sr. was disowned by the Kennet Quaker meeting for taking up arms. In 1780, Isaac married the senior Cloud's daughter Elizabeth (a "non-member" because of her father's status), in a ceremony officiated by a Baptist minister. That double offense was noted as the reason for ejecting Isaac from the Quaker fold.[9]

Isaac Peirce, Abner Cloud Jr., and Abner's brother Amos started working together in the future territory of Washington, still part of the state of Maryland, in the mid-1780s. Besides escaping unfriendly Chester County, Peirce and the Clouds also may have decided the county was too crowded and open land too scarce. Isaac may have financed his initial property acquisitions with assistance from his Cloud in-laws, since his family in Pennsylvania had limited resources. In 1764, Peirce's father owned or rented about four hundred acres in Chester County and had a quarter interest in a saw mill.[10] As a third-born son whose two brothers and two sisters survived to middle age or older, Isaac received only a modest inheritance (his father died in 1803 and his mother in 1810, leaving him 105 pounds and three silver dollars, respectively).

Despite wartime setbacks, in the early 1780s the Cloud family, joining sometimes with the Peirces and other investors and speculators, began a property-buying spree that ranged over three states. The informal syndicate owned land just west of Georgetown, on the north

The restored Abner Cloud House on
the C & O Canal in Washington, D.C.
Photograph by Steve Dryden, 2008.

banks of the Potomac in what was then Maryland. A Virginia land grant of 1786 (in today's West Virginia, southwest of Morgantown) refers to "Abner Clouds survey" adjoining the land. By the mid-1790s, the family owned land on Rock Creek, and at the same time was buying and selling tracts of land between Philadelphia and Baltimore. At one point, the Clouds held ten thousand acres as part of another speculative investment in western Virginia.[11]

Peirce, meanwhile, took advantage of the business opportunities offered by a nascent city. During the late 1790s, as construction continued on the new capital, Isaac contracted with the Commissioners of Public Buildings, who used small boats to ship plaster up Rock Creek to be ground at his mill. Whether he built a separate facility for plaster milling is unknown, but over the course of the nineteenth century waterpower would be used to run a sawmill, too.[12]

Always on the lookout for more land, Isaac Peirce bought four acres at the mouth of Piney Branch, on the east side of Rock Creek—between present-day D.C. communities of Crestwood and Mount Pleasant—a few months before his purchase of the mill in 1794. By 1798, business had evolved enough for citizens to petition the Maryland General Assembly for a road to run near his mill to a landing below the locks of a new Potomac Company canal along the river, west of the new city. In "dry seasons, the neighborhood can calculate that the grain necessary to support their families will be ground . . ." at Peirce's mill, the petition said.[13]

By 1791, the Clouds and their in-laws had exclusive title to land at what was then known as Woodward's Cove (now Fletcher's Boathouse). Abner Cloud Jr. settled on the property sometime in the late 1790s, marrying Susanna Pimmett Smallwood, whose father, William Smallwood, owned adjacent land. The house Cloud built of grey fieldstone still stands and bears the inscription "AC 1801," chiseled in a rock in the attic chimney structure, indicating the year building was completed. Apparently, the mill went up around the same time.

The Cloud house has three stories, the first floor featuring what was probably a dining room, with floor-to-ceiling china cabinets. The kitchen was in the basement, entered through a door on the ground level. The kitchen includes a stone-lined oven, and a large fireplace, six feet wide and four feet high, typical of that era.[*]

The Cloud mill stood at the eastern terminus of the Potomac Company canal, built to bypass the Potomac River's Little Falls and other obstacles to navigation. The vision of the Potomac Company, which George Washington founded in 1784, was to connect Georgetown and Alexandria with the Ohio River and Pittsburgh. The proprietors' first effort was a series of canals skirting the river's rapids. Cloud was among the investors and speculators who bought land in the area as Washington's public venture was getting underway. In 1785, Washington and an entourage canoed downriver from Harper's Ferry to Little Falls, portaging around the perilous Great Falls, to conduct a personal inspection of the proposed trade route.

The Potomac Company project was completed in 1795—two locks were named "George" and "Martha"—but despite being a major engineering success, it ultimately failed as a commercial venture. Trade with the West was growing, but much of the year the river ran too low for upstream travel. The canal made little money and finally shut down in 1828. Its successor, the Chesapeake and Ohio Canal, was built as one continuous conduit along the Potomac, stretching all the way to Cumberland, Maryland.[14]

[*]The Abner Cloud house is now owned by the National Park Service. It was restored and furnished during the American Bicentennial by the Colonial Dames of America and is periodically opens to visitors. Nothing remains of the mill complex except a foundation, rubble, and a hint of the millrace.

Ruins of the Cloud mill. Photograph from the Rambler collection, ca. 1914.
Courtesy Historical Society of Washington, D.C.

Cloud benefited from a court decision in 1792 against the Potomac Company's claim that it owned surplus water not used in the canal. That enabled Cloud to use the excess water to run his mill wheel. His business seems to have initially prospered, partly because of the mill's convenient location along the canal. Cloud had the leisure time and the disposable income to indulge in one of the gentry's favorite pastimes, horse racing. In a newspaper article published in April 1802, Cloud boasted of a colt he owned that was an offspring of "Driver," a famed English racehorse: "This colt leapt at 2 years old over a fence, & deep gully in the presence of several witnesses, and the leap was correctly measured . . . and found to be 24 feet on the level." That same year, President Thomas Jefferson appointed Cloud a lieutenant in the District of Columbia militia.

Cloud also did well enough that he eventually could pay an overseer and buy several slaves, in addition to supporting his wife and five children. As the son of a disowned Quaker, Cloud did not have to follow the sect's ban on slave-holding. He leased two, one-hundred-acre plots that he owned along the Potomac to individuals in the fishing trade. Cloud's house was furnished with Windsor chairs, a mahogany table, silver service items, and wine decanters.[15]

A local Washington historian, inspired by the Cloud saga, composed this appealing scene in a mid-1920s essay:

> The tall, three-storied (Cloud) house, with the wide, old fashioned chimney, faced the river, to which the land sloped gently, unbroken by either canal or railway, and undefaced by summer shacks. On the other hand, the mill, with its racing water, kept up a pleasant clatter. Abner Cloud, looking homeward from the mill, had a most agreeable view through the trees of his house (to the cove) where little pleasure boats were tied or larger boats bringing traffic for the mill were anchored. Out in the main stream of the river was an ever-moving procession of sailboats on trading errands up and down the Potomac valley. Turning into the canal just above the mill, their white wings might be seen from the Cloud house, floating through the trees toward the falls.[16]

However, by the time Cloud died, during the last weeks of 1812, he was deep in debt. Court records contain numerous IOUs for cash signed by Cloud, and large bills from merchants for everything from blacksmithing services to sugar and whiskey (sixty-five gallons of the latter bought during 1809 to 1810; the liquor may have been used to compensate workers). His balance sheet easily could be upset by the weather. The day before Christmas in 1811, Cloud asked a creditor for more time because the frozen Potomac had delayed his anticipated income from a shipment of wood downstream.

Cloud's last dunning notices include bills for the purchase of 130 pounds of flour and barrels of corn, oats, and rye, but the documents make no direct references to the mill.

PUBLIC SALE.

Pursuant to an order from the orphans court for Washington county, District of Columbia, will be sold at public auction, on Thursday the 25th of February, if fair, if not, the next fair day, at the late residence of Abner Cloud, deceased,

The following articles :

A large quantity of well conditioned TO-BACCO in bulk, fit for packing and prising

A number of valuable NEGROES, consisting of two young men, two young women, one woman and child

Two valuable Studs, and six other Horses

Waggon Cart and Harness

Five Milch Cows, Sixteen Hogs.

Fifteen barrels of Fish

Between 5 and 600 bushels Salt

3 Seins, 3 Boats & fishing tackle complete

21 Hogsheads and sundry Empty Casks

A quantity of Farming Utensils, Household Furniture, &c too tedious to enumerate

The terms of sale are— for all sums under twenty dollars, cash ; for all sums over twenty dollars, a credit of six months will be given, the purchasers to give their notes with approved endorsers, with interest from the day of sale.

SUSANNA R. CLOUD, adm'x
EVERARD GARY adm'
J. TRAVERS, Auct.

Feb. uary 3   law 4

Notice for auction of Abner Cloud's property. *Courtesy Library of Congress.*

At one point, Cloud may have leased the operation to a miller, but by 1812, the year he died, he no longer owned the mill. Evidently he was forced to sell it because of his dire financial situation.

In his final years, Cloud sold large quantities of herring and other fish, which were plentiful in the Potomac in those days. Labor for this commercial fishery came from slaves owned by others. Contracting for such services was a standard practice in that era, and Cloud's debts included bills for these labor arrangements. A few weeks before his death, a District court issued an arrest warrant for Cloud's failure to pay an unspecified debt of $8.41. Though it is unclear whether this order was carried out, it was an undignified ending for the son of an upwardly mobile family.

In February 1813, two months after Cloud's death, a District probate court ordered the sale of six persons, including a child, who had been enslaved by Cloud, and eight horses, as well as "a large quantity of well conditioned tobacco," fifteen barrels of fish, more than five hundred bushels of salt, and three boats. The Clouds' household furniture also went on the auction block. The sale brought in more than $2,500, but Cloud's estate remained mired in court proceedings for years.[17]

Susanna Cloud remained at the canal house with her children. About two years after her husband's death, she remarried a Maryland farmer named William Roberts. She apparently still owned 248 acres of land in Fairfax County, Virginia, and in an effort to defray her late husband's debts, she advertised it for sale in late 1813.[18] Abner and Susanna Cloud's son briefly attended Georgetown College. Two of the Clouds' daughters would later marry men from the locally prominent Carbery family.

Jonathan Shoemaker kept the Quaker faith when he moved from Philadelphia to the new American capital, though he seems not to have been doctrinaire, for he paid taxes during at least one year of the Revolution, a deviation followed by one of his brothers who joined the Philadelphia County militia.[19] Jonathan was accepted by his coreligionists in Washington, becoming a leading member of their small community. In 1807, Shoemaker donated land near his "Columbia" mill on Rock Creek to be the Quaker cemetery.*

But one of Shoemaker's commercial ventures came to an embarrassingly un-Quakerish end. Through the capital's Quaker network, Shoemaker became acquainted with President Jefferson. U.S. Commissioner of Patents William Thornton was a Quaker, and Dolley Madison, the wife of Jefferson's secretary of state, James Madison, also had been brought up in the faith. Dolley knew Shoemaker's second wife, Elizabeth, from childhood in their native Philadelphia, and is said to have visited Elizabeth occasionally at the Shoemaker mill on Rock Creek. Jefferson needed operators for the mills on his Shadwell property, south of Monticello, and Thornton recommended Shoemaker, who agreed to rent them.[20]

Jonathan delegated his twenty-five-year-old son, Isaac, to run the Jefferson mills. Trained by his father's assistants, Isaac began work at Shadwell late in 1806, when the mills still were being built. The operation suffered setbacks early on, first from a severe drought that reduced potential waterpower, and then from violent thunderstorms that destroyed the mill's dam. To complicate matters, Isaac alienated Jefferson's adult daughter, Martha Randolph, who was living at Monticello. In March 1809, Martha wrote Jefferson, who was then ending his presidency, that Isaac was "not a man of business" and "has not one speck of honesty." It "would be better for you to get the mill back upon any terms," she wrote, adding, "I am afraid you have been deceived in the character of his (Isaac's) Father."[21] Isaac Shoemaker never made enough money at the mills to pay Jefferson the $1,250 annual rent.

Jonathan Shoemaker's family preferred to recall his relationship with Jefferson as one of mutual esteem, and maintained that Jonathan bent over backwards to make the mill business work when disputes arose. "It has always been a maxim of my life to suffer rather than contend," Shoemaker is said to have remarked during a meeting with Jefferson over business matters. "Mr. Shoemaker," Jefferson replied, "I think I can go as far . . . as you can."[22]

Jefferson held a favorable view of Quakers and remained cordial with Jonathan Shoemaker, but the third president's own finances never were solid, to say the least. By 1810, he was sending Jonathan Shoemaker letters from creditors to illustrate his desperation. "It has been a sincere affliction for me to be so importunate with you on the subject of my rents," Jefferson wrote, "but my necessities have forced it on me." They agreed to sever their business ties that year. To pay the debts, Jonathan had to sell the Columbia mill on Rock Creek, and his shares in a Washington-Richmond stagecoach line that he owned with another Quaker entrepreneur, Nathaniel Ellicott.[23]

As Shoemaker and Abner Cloud struggled to make ends meet, Isaac Peirce's mill and farm prospered, and Peirce began taking a series of low-profile civic positions in the new capital. It was a role that he and others in his family would play for years to come.

---

* This area is between Calvert Street and Adams Mill Road, just east of present-day Rock Creek Park. In the late nineteenth century, it became an important African-American burial ground. Later, the area was developed as an apartment complex and playground known as the Walter Peirce Park. Apparently, there is no relation between Walter Peirce and the Peirces of this chronicle.

2

A Mill and Twenty Thousand Apple Trees

IN 1800, WASHINGTON, D.C., officially became the capital of the United States of America. Boats arrived at Georgetown in late spring, bearing records and papers shipped from Philadelphia, the most recent temporary seat of government. During a brief visit in June, President John Adams encountered beautiful countryside on the outskirts of the Washington settlement—and dismally little else. A ten-year promotional campaign intended to lure buyers and builders to the new city had failed, and the unpaved avenues were lined not with grand mansions but shacks. Work on federal office buildings barely had begun, and the president's house was yet unfinished. "Melancholy and ludicrous . . . a city in ruins," was one congressman's assessment.[1]

Isaac Peirce may have shared this pessimistic view, but his activities beyond the farm and mill concerned matters of local governance, not federal affairs. In May 1802, newly elected President Jefferson named Peirce to the Levy Court, which acted as a board of commissioners for Washington County, the area outside the formal urban core laid out by French planner Peter Charles L'Enfant. To attend Levy Court meetings, Peirce rode more than two miles on horseback from his home to the embryonic city. Other members of the court—a key position for any ambitious businessman, since that body determined tax assessments and built roads—included building contractor Robert Brent (who also served as Washington's first mayor), Daniel Carroll, of the prominent local landowning family, Georgetown tobacco heir Thomas Peter, and manufacturer and future Georgetown mayor Thomas Corcoran. In the first week of January 1803, after the holiday revels, Peirce and his fellow Levy Court members issued a sober call for a public meeting, no doubt to discuss how the small community would handle its financial affairs.[2]

Two years later, in 1805, Isaac Peirce joined Jefferson and dozens of other prominent citizens urging the establishment of a "permanent institution for the education of youth in Washington City." Peirce promised twenty dollars to the new school (the highest pledge was

Jefferson's $200). The idea of a free public school was novel in the new country—until that time, only the wealthy could afford to educate their children, usually with private tutors. Within a year, two small schoolhouses were built, supplemented by the creation of a Lancaster-style educational institution, which was named after the English Quaker who originated the idea of using older students as teachers for younger ones to promote wider learning.[3]

School trustees recruited Henry Ould, the son of an English inventor, and brought him to the capital to head the Lancaster school. Within a few years Ould would marry Isaac Peirce's granddaughter, Elizabeth, whom he may have met after Peirce advertised in a local newspaper, the *National Intelligencer,* for a tutor for his children.[4] One account says Elizabeth Peirce was "bewitchingly pretty," and "rode to and fro [around the Peirce farmlands] in an ancient coach, whose doors are said to have borne the blazoning of the Peirce [coat of] arms."[5]

Isaac was named trustee of what seems to have been a combined school and church, established in the rural area between his home and Georgetown for the "benefit of the neighborhood, and for a place of public worship for all denominations of Christians . . . ."[6] As a prominent landowner, Peirce also became active in one of the first farmers' associations in the capital. He was among the judges at an exhibition of the Columbian Agricultural Society in May 1812, held at the "elegant lot of woodland belonging to Thomas Beall," builder of the Dumbarton estate in Georgetown. The other judges included several members of Congress.[7]

The War of 1812 between Britain and the United States culminated in the British rampage through Washington, in which Redcoat troops burned the Capitol, the White House, and other public buildings—an event that further impeded the lagging effort to fulfill L'Enfant's plan for a grand capital. If the Peirces sometimes suffered from their relative isolation in a roadless area of Washington County, during the British incursion that handicap proved a blessing. In August 1814, the invaders entered from the east on the Bladensburg Turnpike, torched whatever government structures they could identify in Washington City, and less than forty-eight hours later withdrew via the same route, never approaching the Peirce farmstead.

In December 1814, Peirce advertised in local newspapers that he had twenty thousand apple trees for sale.[8] He continued to expand his holdings along Rock Creek, and sometime before 1817, he bought a shoreline "fishing landing" at Little Falls, near the mill that his late brother-in-law Abner Cloud had built. A neighboring landowner granted Peirce the right to pass through his property on the condition that the pathway "be the width of a common waggon road and at all times shall be free to all carts, waggons."[9] Long before Europeans arrived, native Americans had favored the spot, drawn especially by each spring's spawning run. English explorer John Smith, who reached the Little Falls area in 1607, wrote that near the falls, "neither better fish, more plenty, nor more variety for smal fish, had any of vs euer seene in any place so swimming in the water."[10] Isaac could lease the landing to commercial fishermen, as salted fish was a staple during the winter months. Being cheap

Peirce Mill, ca. 1830, artist unknown. This painting apparently was done shortly after construction of the mill building that still stands today at Rock Creek and Tilden Street. Note the ford across Rock Creek, the small waterwheel on the right side of the mill building, and what could have been the miller's log cabin, across the road on the left. *Courtesy Theodore R. Hazen Jr.*

The Peirce springhouse in 1936. Built in 1801, it is still standing on Tilden Street, west of the mill.
Courtesy Library of Congress Prints and Photographs Division.

and plentiful, fish served as food for enslaved African Americans, and could be ground up for use as fertilizer.

Peirce's expansion of operations on his Rock Creek property began around 1800, when he built a saw mill. A springhouse followed, along with a potato house and cow barn, carriage house, distillery (he brewed fruit-based brandies), and miller's house. He capped the enlargement of his farmstead in 1829, by completing the substantial stone mill building that still stands alongside Rock Creek. At least that is the presumption, based on the initials and date "BIP 1829" cut into the stone at the south gable. The rune could be an abbreviation for "Betsy and Isaac Peirce" or "Built by Isaac Peirce."[11]

It certainly would be accurate to read the inscription as referring to Isaac Peirce. He numbered, among his many skills, those of millwright, or one who builds mills. But he did not do the milling himself. As he grew wealthier, Peirce used slave labor, and he may have assigned the miller's role to an African-American man, while he focused on managing his farm and carrying out civic duties in Washington County. Eventually, the Peirce family

The Peirce carriage house, ca. 1975 (sign refers to mill hidden at right).
Courtesy National Park Service.

would lease the structure to a miller who did the work and paid an annual rent. Peirce apparently grew little wheat but both he and his neighbors would have needed the grain for flour and bread production. Cornmeal was another mainstay, and other cereals were grown for fodder.

Wheat grew well at the edge of the Piedmont, where soils were more suited to that crop than the Tidewater's earlier mainstay, tobacco. In addition, it made more financial sense to trade in wheat, since, once ground into flour, it was a compact, more easily transported commodity. Farmers followed the same logic when distilling liquor from various grains. By 1810, milling was Washington's second most important manufacturing enterprise, with annual production valued at more than $200,000.[12]

Milling in that period was intensely local. In 1810, Pennsylvania supported more than 2,000 mills; Virginia, 441.[13] Rock Creek's numerous mills dotted the stream deep into Maryland, as well as in the District of Columbia. These Rock Creek mills (and most mills in the mid-Atlantic region) were small, so-called custom mills, serving farmers whose land lay within a few miles of the waterwheel. Output normally did not top fifty barrels a day. Plagued by poor roads and lacking navigable waters, these mill owners had no hope of growth that would allow them to compete with mills that exported their production on the Potomac River and other major waterways. One mill historian sketched a quaint scene of a custom mill, where the farmers would "bring their grain to the miller, wait around exchanging opinions and smoking while he ground their grain into meal or flour, and then grumble that he took an unfair amount of his hard-earned crop [as payment]."[14]

Isaac built his two-thousand-square-foot mill's exterior of blue-gray and brown stone, presumably quarried by the Peirces on land they owned upstream near Rock Creek's Piney or Broad Branch tributaries. The base stones, thirty inches thick, taper to twenty-three inches at the roof level. "Primly symmetrical and solid," as one Rock Creek Park study put it, this conservative style undoubtedly reflects Isaac's exposure to the stonework of German immigrants in Pennsylvania, where he was raised. It also has classic elements of the boxy Federal and Georgian styles popular in the era. Simple rectangular windows were spaced equidistant around the building; inside, oak and pine made up the framing and three floors. Other surviving Peirce farm buildings show the same utilitarian style. They were built to last.[15]

The mill sits on a slope, about one hundred feet west of Rock Creek. To turn the millwheel, water had to be brought from upstream, alongside the creek, in a channel called a headrace. The power that can be derived from a waterwheel is constrained by head, the vertical distance from the water level above the wheel to the water level below, and flow, the quantity of water that can be consistently diverted from a stream to the waterwheel. The head at Rock Creek mill sites was a challenge for millwrights, who would have preferred steeper grades along the creek for a taller head. Flow was sufficient but seasonally inconsistent.

Nineteenth-century maps show that about three hundred feet north of the mill, a dam diverted water into the headrace. Another map shows a headrace extending more than one thousand feet upstream, to the Broad Branch tributary on the creek's western shore. Isaac Peirce and owners of other mills on Rock Creek no doubt experimented with

A cutaway diagram showing the automated operation at Peirce Mill using Oliver Evans' innovations: (1) Miller dumps grain into receiving hopper on first floor; (2) Water flowing down headrace makes waterwheel turn; (3) Wooden gears in basement engage to turn the main shaft, which powers other parts in the mill; (4) Scoops on continuous belt carry grain to attic where wire cylinder strains impurities and shakes grain into chute; (5) Chute carries grain to bin on second floor that feeds grindstone; (6) Top runner stone on the first floor revolves one-sixteenth inch above stationary bed stone to crack kernels; (7) Flour drops off edge of stone and passes into chute; (8) Elevator carries flour to attic where "hopper boy" mechanism stirs and cools; (9) Chute carries flour to bolter (sifter) on second floor, then to bin where it is bagged. *Drawing by Theodore R. Hazen Jr.*

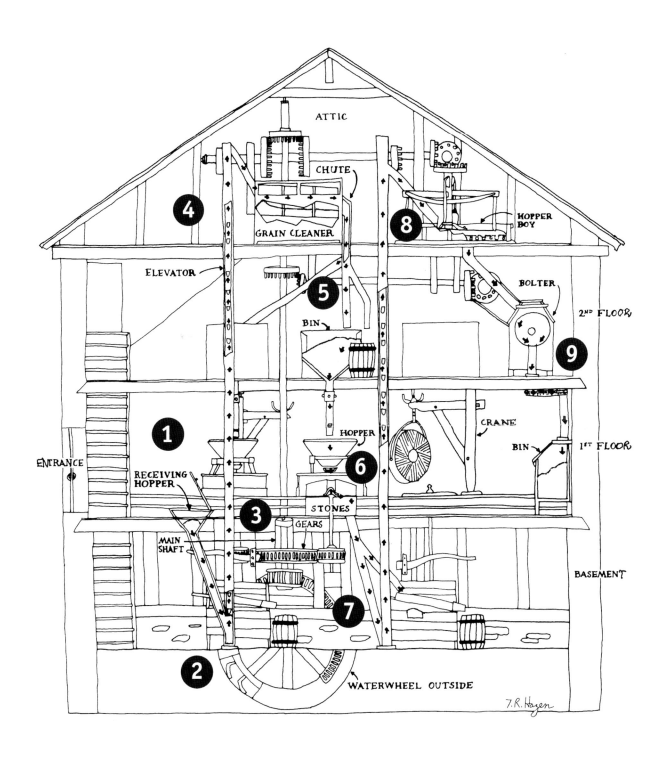

ATTIC

CHUTE

④ GRAIN CLEANER

⑧ HOPPER BOY

ELEVATOR

⑤ BOLTER 2ND FLOOR

BIN

⑨

① HOPPER

ENTRANCE ⑥ CRANE

RECEIVING HOPPER 1ST FLOOR

BIN

STONES

③ GEARS

MAIN SHAFT BASEMENT

⑦

②

WATERWHEEL OUTSIDE

T. R. Hazen

varying headrace designs, since they had other problems to cope with besides topography. Flash floods, caused by the clearing of land much farther upstream in Washington and Montgomery County, imperiled the mill dam and the mill building itself.

Peirce also tried different types of waterwheels. Millwrights used three basic designs. In the undershot, water passed under the wheel in a flow just high enough to strike paddles mounted on the wheel, turning it. This configuration was only marginally efficient, but worked well enough in times of low water. The most efficient designs were the breast wheel, which caught the water near the middle of the wheel, and the overshot, which used the weight of water pouring out of a trough onto the top of the wheel. The most current engineering study of the mill concludes that Isaac may have begun, in 1829, with an undershot wheel, perhaps replaced later in the century by versions of the other two options. But the low head from Rock Creek would have made the wheel diameter smaller than optimal, thus limiting its efficiency. The ongoing success of Peirce's mill, despite nearby commercial rivals, suggests that Peirce and his millers managed the vagaries of water flow with a combination of design innovations and good business habits.[17] It is also likely that Isaac improved his enterprise by adopting revolutionary technology pioneered by American inventor Oliver Evans.

In Georgetown, mill owners took advantage of the greater waterpower of the Potomac River and access to the harbor to expand their businesses. Isaac Peirce was not interested in merging with one of those companies, nor did he want to move to a riverfront location. He was satisfied with the farmstead on Rock Creek, of which the mill was just one component. Not surprisingly, his family would be joined to another Quaker clan in the capital that was deeply involved in the milling industry.

Oliver Evans, ca. 1813. *Courtesy Hagley Museum.*

A DELAWARE NATIVE, Oliver Evans grew up at the center of the mid-Atlantic milling industry. First apprenticed to a wagon-maker, Evans later joined his brothers in their mill business. By 1785, when he turned thirty, constant experimenting led Evans to devise an automated milling system. Evans's opus, *The Young Mill-Wright & Miller's Guide* (1795), describes how grain cleaners, bolting screens, and elevators—operated by belts and gears driven by the vertical shaft attached to the water-wheel—could effect a dramatic reduction in the back-breaking labor for which the traditional mill was notorious. No longer would the miller and his helpers have to haul bags of grain upstairs for grinding or afterwards carry bags of flour from the basement. Flour made from using the Evans system was also cleaner, and his detailed manual even offers advice on bookkeeping and labor efficiency. All in all, the improvements that Evans promulgated were said to boost productivity sevenfold. Though it is impossible, without further evidence, to say how much of the Evans system Isaac Peirce incorporated, it would have been uncharacteristic of the man not to have put such innovation to use.

Evans never achieved the fame of Samuel Morse or other inventors from that era, despite having made two major technological breakthroughs—the other being the high-pressure steam engine. One reason for this relative obscurity could have been his personality. Though he aggressively defended his patents in court as he pursued licensing fees, and hungered for public recognition, he burned a large batch of his technical papers during a fit of pique, lest they fall into the hands of those he deemed unscrupulous rivals. "Pompous blockhead" was one of many uncomplimentary descriptions given him during his lifetime, and even a sympathetic biographer admits Evans was "abrasive" and "querulous," and "deserved much of the hostility he aroused."[16]

3

The Peirce-Shoemaker Connection

IN ADDITION TO THE UNFORTUNATE MILLER, Isaac Shoemaker, whose activities after working at Thomas Jefferson's Shadwell establishment were impossible to trace, Jonathan Shoemaker had four other sons. George Shoemaker, the most successful, was named flour inspector of Georgetown in 1816, the year he turned twenty-four. Although situated within the federal city, Georgetown had its own municipal government and created the flour-inspector post in 1808, an acknowledgment that the milling industry had become a key part of the local economy. Shoemaker's skill at grading flour and ensuring a quality product was of such renown that Georgetown's brands were "demanded in all parts of the country," a history of the family noted.[1]

George Shoemaker maintained his parents' Quaker traditions; one sign of his filial devotion was a return to his family's Philadelphia-area community to seek a Quaker bride. He did this twice, the second time after his first wife died at a young age. His second wife, Elizabeth Lukens Shoemaker, became clerk and treasurer of the Washington Quaker meeting; her other faith-based duties included directing, as a volunteer, the Union of the Benevolent Society and the Female Orphans Society. George, too, was active in civic affairs—as guardian of the Georgetown School, serving on the Board of Health, and acting as city warden. He also organized Georgetown's first volunteer fire company. In business, he owned the Riverside Mill, a medium-sized operation on Water (today's K) Street, which produced one hundred barrels of flour a day of all grades. Meanwhile, he rose through management of the Farmers and Mechanics Bank of Georgetown to become its president. Politically, he was a leader in the local Whig Party, opposed to the populist politics of Democrat Andrew Jackson.[2]

George Shoemaker Inspecting Flour for the Port of Georgetown, by James Alexander Simpson, 1840.
Courtesy National Portrait Gallery, Smithsonian Institution; Gift of the Estate of William Woodville VIII.

David Shoemaker Sr., brother of Jonathan Shoemaker, undated. *Courtesy Chester County Historical Society.*

Painting of David Shoemaker Jr., son-in-law of Isaac Peirce and father of Pierce Shoemaker, ca. 1815. *Courtesy Historical Society of Washington, D.C.*

George Shoemaker remained the town flour inspector for the rest of his life. A portrait from 1840 shows him on the Georgetown wharf surrounded by flour barrels, dressed in top hat and waistcoat, and holding a stick used to sample the flour. His lips are pursed and his eyes narrowed.

Shoemaker's worldly success can be seen in the fact that in the early 1860s, his personal net worth approached $500,000, if the sum is adjusted for inflation. His house at 3116 P Street, NW, was furnished comfortably and reveals a sophisticated lifestyle.[3] He evidently was regarded as a fair and judicious man, and had a talent for arranging the necessary modus vivendi, for no record could be found of any challenge to his conflict of interest in inspecting competitors' flour output. There were at least five non-Shoemaker mills in Georgetown in the mid-nineteenth century.

It was through George Shoemaker's uncle, David Shoemaker Sr., that Isaac Peirce's family and the Shoemakers became related by marriage. Being so intimately involved in the local world of wheat, milling, and flour—and sharing a Quaker background—the Peirces were no doubt familiar to the Shoemakers as both families prospered in the new capital. David Shoemaker, born in 1755 near Philadelphia, joined a local militia during the Revolution; it is unknown whether he was ejected from his Quaker meeting for that action. By the mid-1790s, he was working at the federal government's General Post Office in Philadelphia. When that department moved to Washington in 1800, Shoemaker followed, serving as a clerk to the postmaster general. He kept the job for the next two decades, and in 1821, was earning $1,000 annually. The department was housed in the Blodgett Hotel on E Street, NW, where Shoemaker and two dozen other men oversaw the country's 4,500 post offices and 73,000 miles of postal routes. The General Post Office was one of the early centers of political intrigue in Washington. The postmaster general had the power to appoint local postmasters and other employees; consequently, he wielded enormous patronage power— and attracted numerous congressional investigations.[4]

With his steady income, Shoemaker managed to save enough money to invest in property in Washington City, and his reputation was such that in 1814, the city's aldermen appointed him to be an election commissioner. Shoemaker enjoyed a comparatively long life, and though still vigorous enough in his late sixties to swim in the Potomac, he drowned

Peirce Mill, 1855. Naturalist and artist Titian Ramsey Peale, son of noted Philadelphia painter Charles Willson Peale, took this photograph, which also partially shows the carriage house and a barn. Peale, who worked at the U.S. Patent Office in Washington, experimented with the wet-plate method, an early photographic technique. His album labeled the mill image: "T R Peales first attempt at photography." *Courtesy Smithsonian National Museum of American History.*

Panorama from Pierce's Heights (detail), by Alexander H. Clements, 1848.
This painting apparently shows a view looking south, to the Potomac River,
from the Linnaean Hill area. *Courtesy Albert Small.*

there while cooling off with friends on a July afternoon in 1825. Two days later, the *National Intelligencer* published an obituary that mourned him as an "esteemed and respected fellow-citizen" and "faithful public servant."[5]

President John Quincy Adams was also in the habit of taking a daily swim in the river, close to the same place where Shoemaker drowned. The morning after the accident, he came upon the search party, and later wrote in his diary that one member of the rescue group had said that "he had never seen a more distressed person than Mrs. Shoemaker last evening," after being informed that her husband was missing. Adams witnessed the discovery of Shoemaker's body within a few minutes of his arrival at the river bank.[6]

Shoemaker's son, David Shoemaker Jr., born in 1795, served in the Washington, D.C., militia during the War of 1812, then ran a hardware store on Pennsylvania Avenue. A portrait painted of David as a young man, perhaps still in his teens, shows him to be handsome, dark-haired, and serious. He is formally dressed in a white shirt with a flared collar, a light-colored vest, and a dark cravat. The painting could show him as his wedding approached, since on the last day of 1815, a Presbyterian minister presided over a ceremony in which the twenty-year-old Shoemaker wed Abigail Peirce (the youngest daughter of Isaac Peirce), who was barely seventeen. The next year, Abigail Shoemaker bore their first child, named Pierce Shoemaker.[7]

Within a few years, David's hardware business failed, but unlike his cousin Isaac Shoemaker, he was not rescued by his father. Nor, it seems, was he helped very much by his new in-laws, the Peirces, though their milling and farming businesses were growing. The lack of support could suggest strained relations with his in-laws. In any event, David did time in the city debtors' prison. After his release, he took a more secure job in the federal government's land office, which surveyed and sold public land in the West and administered the Homestead Act. He evidently spent the rest of his working life there.[8]

Isaac Peirce died in 1841, at the age of about eighty-five (his wife, Elizabeth, had died in 1833). At that point, the mill was only one of numerous money-making enterprises on Isaac's large farmstead. He operated a distillery, raised sheep, pigs, and milk cows, and grew potatoes, wheat, rye, and oats. As a major landholder in Washington, Peirce owned what one family member later estimated at two thousand acres in various parcels along Rock Creek and elsewhere.[9]

Isaac's will, written in 1825, alludes to some tension in the household over his estate. In it, he urged his children to promote "brotherly and sisterly love and affection toward each other," as that "is among the last and greatest desires that a fond and affectionate father leaves." Isaac wrote that he did not want to "express any opinion" about the "terms upon which they [the children] may . . . live together." Nevertheless, he concluded, "it is to be understood that I leave my son Abner the whole and entire right to all of my property," except for items Isaac bequeathed to children and grandchildren. Indeed, Isaac's first son,

Abner, then fifty-six, inherited the mill on Rock Creek and most of the land. A total of $7,850 was distributed among children and grandchildren.[10]

Abner and his sister Elizabeth Cloud Peirce continued to live at the Peirce family home. No record exists showing that either one ever married. They were "alienated from" the rest of the family, one acquaintance said, without giving details. Their younger brother, Job, died relatively young, while the other siblings who grew to adulthood married and in some cases moved out of the Washington area. Abner and Elizabeth,* also known as "Miss Betsy," were very close. A neighbor recalled that Elizabeth vowed "to do all she could for him [Abner] while she lived, and that his was hers and hers was his referring to property." Despite being obese—one source puts her weight in the unlikely region of 400 to 450 pounds—and having African-American servant girls, Elizabeth was an "early riser" and "very industrious," sometimes seen mending clothes and ironing, work then deemed beneath the station of a woman who had servants. "She was remarkably economical in her dress and had no expensive habits," a close family friend said. "She did not visit anywhere."[11]

In October 1846, a *National Intelligencer* correspondent spent a day walking the "winding vale" in the mill's vicinity. His account is one of autumnal bliss—boys looking for chestnuts, men mashing apples into cider, and fresh fish from the creek available for sale. The writer asked some of the boys where he might have the catch cooked, and one of them pointed to a home on the side of the hill.

"On our arrival there we were warmly welcomed," the correspondent recalled, "and in due time we had the satisfaction of enjoying as finely cooked fish as ever tickled the palate of Izaak Walton . . . . Not only were we waited upon with marked politeness, but were treated with an abundance of currant wine, and for all this truly southern hospitality we could make no return, except in the way of gratitude."

The correspondent was even more struck by the vine- and moss-covered "cottage" where he enjoyed his meal. "It struck me as one of the most comfortable and poetical nooks that I ever beheld. It seemed to have everything about it calculated to win the heart of a lover of nature and the rural life."[12] The writer was referring to the old Peirce homestead, then overseen by Abner Peirce. The writer estimated the home to be one hundred years old, which could mean the Peirces lived in a dwelling that existed before they bought the land in the 1790s.

However, it was Isaac's other son, Joshua, ten years younger than Abner, whose house and life would be better remembered.

* There were three women of widely disparate ages named Elizabeth Cloud Peirce in the family during the first decades of the nineteenth century. See the family tree for the relationships among the three.

4

Linnaean Hill

IN 1823, ISAAC PEIRCE GAVE EIGHTY-TWO ACRES along Rock Creek to his son Joshua, then in his mid-twenties and keen on commercial horticulture. It was a vocation laced into the family genes. Joshua had watched his father's tree nursery business grow. Their cousins, Jacob and Samuel Peirce, began an arboretum with varied trees and shrubs that later became Pennsylvania's famed Longwood Gardens. And working with plants suited their Quaker heritage, for a number of the great botanists and plantsmen of the Pennsylvania colony emerged from the Society of Friends. For the Quakers, the investigation of nature was a way to know and understand God.

Besides fruit trees, Isaac's expanding farm operation included cultivation of thorn bushes used to delineate property lines and fence in livestock. He exchanged ideas with an enterprising neighbor and fellow Pennsylvanian in the Rock Creek valley, John Adlum. By 1820, Adlum had established what he called the "Vineyard" on land that is today Cleveland Park, experimenting in making wine from native American grapes.[1]

Joshua Peirce "had the advantage of a good education" and "taste and talent," a cousin recalled. Like many others in the extended family, he returned as a youth to Pennsylvania's Quaker heartland, attending school in Philadelphia. That was where he met his wife, Susan Coates, a bank clerk's daughter. Similar to his father, Joshua Peirce brimmed with commercial imagination. Within months of the formal deeding of the Rock Creek property, Joshua named it Linnaean Hill, after Swedish botanist Carl Linnaeus, creator of the Latin classification system for the natural world. The same year, Joshua published his first catalog, offering fruit and ornamental trees, flowers, and greenhouse plants. One of his favorite greenhouse specimens was the camellia, an Asian shrub that he helped popularize, and which sold for as much as one dollar per plant. His greenhouses "were crowded with bushes densely covered with the bloom of this conspicuously beautiful

Joshua Peirce, horticulturalist and founder of Linnaean Hill and its nursery, undated. *Photograph from private collection.*

flower," the same cousin's account said. Peirce developed a "very fine white" camellia variety "equaled by only a few of the older kind," a horticulture magazine reported in 1842.[2]

In later years, Peirce family members liked to repeat the proud claim that the parks and reservations of Washington "were, to a great extent, stocked from Linnaean Hill."[3] This claim has not been documented, and other suppliers were active, but certainly there was a need in the capital for large quantities of plant material. David Warden, the U.S. consul in Paris, returned to Washington in 1812, after several years abroad, and was shocked by what he saw, writing that the "venerable oaks" and other species, along with shrubs and anything else that got in the way, had been "wantonly destroyed" by "barbarian hands," i.e., the early settlers who used the wood for dwellings and fuel.[4] Civic authorities devoted much of the nineteenth century to repairing the devastation caused by poor planning and greed in the capital's early days.

As a pioneering nurseryman, Joshua Peirce expanded his business into nearby states. He also corresponded with prominent colleagues in the commercial field—most notably, Long Islander William Prince, whose nursery was one of the first in the American colonies. Peirce supplied Prince with seeds of various native trees such as the sweet gum, persimmon, and pawpaw, and flowers such as trillium and ladyslipper, while Prince provided Peirce with ornamental evergreens. Peirce also sold two of North America's more noxious imports, English ivy and multiflora rose. They were seen in those days as a pleasing ornamental vine and useful hedging plant, respectively. Both have come to be loathed by gardeners, landscapers, and park managers.

Since Linnaean Hill was far from many potential customers in the city, by the 1840s Peirce had opened a branch of his nursery on undeveloped land he owned just inside the escarpment, or ridge of the ancient Potomac River flood plain, near today's Florida Avenue. His property, covering what would become six city blocks, was connected to the city by Fourteenth Street to the south, and to Linnaean Hill by the country road that ran north. Slash Run, a Rock Creek tributary now buried, flowed through this property, and probably supplied water to the new nursery.[5]

The enthusiasm shared by Joshua Peirce and his small circle of green friends led to forming a learned group, a practice common among the educated and wealthy of the day. The charter members of the Columbia Horticultural Society, organized in the summer of 1833, included viticulturist John Adlum, former Washington mayor Joseph Gales, and William Seaton, editor of the capital's newspaper of record, the *National Intelligencer.* During the next decade, the society staged annual exhibits at the City Hall of flower, fruits, and vegetables, with Peirce a regular participant. His cousin George Shoemaker, the Georgetown flour inspector, also joined the society, showing his own prize garden products. One summer Shoemaker presented the *National Intelligencer* editors with greengage plums they judged to be of "uncommon size and beauty."[6]

Joshua Peirce's affection for the natural world, and more specifically, the Piedmont woodlands in which he lived, can be seen in a passage from an essay he wrote in the mid-1830s:

> The falls of Rock Creek—whoever heard of the falls of Rock Creek? At the distance of about four miles from the city and within the limits of the District lie these beautiful, wild and romantic falls, unknown and unfrequented, in a deep glen, surrounded by lofty hills on either side, covered with a thick and almost impenetrable forest, as yet undefiled by the woodman's ax. Here this beautiful stream, shut out, as it seems, from the rest of the world, and apparently as yet undiscovered, in the short space of half a mile is dashed over continuous rapids of about one hundred feet.

Peirce seems to be referring to the rapids just upstream from the family's mill. He admits that while he has lived in the vicinity all his life (he was then about forty years old), and was an "ardent admirer of the beauties of nature," he had "never thoroughly explored" the banks of Rock Creek to the north. In another passage, Peirce unconsciously anticipates the eventual creation of the country's first national urban park along Rock Creek at the end of the nineteenth century: "Here, Nature as though expressly for the accommodation of picnic parties, has constructed tables from her everlasting rocks and surrounded them with ottomans that would well adorn the portico or even the parlor of a prince."[7]

Not surprisingly, one of the books in Peirce's library was a 1794 edition of *The Columbian Muse,* a collection of early American poems.[8] And for Peirce and others living in undeveloped Washington County, the woodlands offered a remarkable and inspirational array of attractions for the senses in each season. In spring, when the ephemeral wildflowers push out of the earth, white mayflowers, the yellow trout lily, and the pinkish spring beauty cover the ground. Understory trees such as the spicebush, dogwood, and redbud then bloom. The summer canopy of green from the oaks, poplars, maples, and other large trees shelter the occasional cardinal flower, or, in a break in the forest, the orange butterfly weed. In early fall, the visitor can enjoy numerous varieties of goldenrod and the wood aster's delicate white disks, and sample the pawpaw tree's custardlike fruits. By late October, the waning warmth is supported by the orange, reds, and purples of the dying foliage. The yellow flowers of witch hazel are the last to bloom; afterwards, a winter sky of deep blue is complemented by the sycamore's mottled gray-white bark. On the ground, the only green is provided by the occasional holly, laurel, and Christmas fern.

Joshua Peirce's Linnaean Hill home sat on a bluff just south of his father's mill complex. Like those of the mill, the walls of the house are made from locally quarried blue-gray stone, and family lore maintains that Italian artisans installed the tile and frescos. In Joshua's day, a greenhouse capitalized on the property's southern exposure, and other outbuildings included a springhouse, large stone barn, and gatehouse. A series of winding roads and paths provided westward access to the Georgetown-Rockville Road, and to fords across Rock Creek. One expert saw the influence of American landscape architect Andrew Jackson Downing in the way Peirce "embellished the hilly landscape at Linnaean Hill with picturesque trees and shrubs and created an elaborate system of circular drives and paths." The result was to downplay its character as a nursery, and to transform the "natural setting above Rock Creek into a private park." The area became known as "Peirce's pleasure gardens."[9]

THE VARIETIES OF FRUIT TREES and bushes maintained by Joshua Peirce appears extraordinarily large to today's consumer, but such breadth was normal in the eighteenth and nineteenth centuries, when orchardists and the public relished a floral diversity developed over the centuries. Peirce's catalog of 1857 lists approximately fifty varieties of eating and cider apples, forty kinds of peaches, seventy varieties of pears, thirty kinds of cherries, and twenty-five apricot hybrids (the year before, he had advertised twenty thousand peach trees for sale). Among the grape offerings is the native Northern Muscadine, which Peirce calls a "superior fox grape, cultivated at New Lannon [Pa.] for wine, highly recommended by the Shakers." Peirce was known for his talents in fruit cultivation, which included tropical species such as oranges and lemons raised in his greenhouse. Peirce suggested that plots of peach trees be interplanted with corn, potatoes, or other vegetables to achieve a larger, better yield. He does not mention the best fruit for making brandy, though reputedly the Peirces made fine liquor at their own distillery.[10]

Linnaean Hill, home of Joshua Peirce, ca. 1875. Today it is known as the Klingle Mansion.
Courtesy Historical Society of Washington, D.C.

Along with his devotion to horticulture, Joshua Peirce followed his father in taking a largely unheralded role in the governance of Washington County. He spent at least ten years on the county's Levy Court, a quasi-governing body, and on several juries for criminal trials. His Levy Court duties, which often involved routine pension and other administrative matters, could also serve the interests of large landowners—including his family's. One example concerned a motion to study a new county road in the vicinity of Linnaean Hill and Peirce Mill. Joshua's cousin, Lewis Carbery, the Washington surveyor and another Levy Court member, proposed that he, Peirce, and another local landowner, Benjamin French, constitute the committee that would undertake the study. The court, including Peirce and Carbery, voted to approve the motion.[11]

On the first day of May 1845, Joshua Peirce and other Levy Court justices paid a ceremonial visit to President James K. Polk at the White House.[12] In the still-small circles of Washington's permanent society, Peirce was strengthening his stature. Politically, Peirce was at one time active in the city's "Jackson Republican" party faction, apparently after

Farmhouse at the Fourteenth Street branch of Joshua Peirce's nursery.
Drawing by Delancey Gill, 1882. *Courtesy Historical Society of Washington, D.C.*

populist Andrew Jackson's victory over the incumbent president, John Quincy Adams, in 1828 (Polk, too, was a Jackson supporter). The Jackson Republican faction was known for opposing high protective tariffs, and a powerful federal government that would include a national bank. But arguments over these questions, though emotional at times, soon would be eclipsed by the issue of slavery. That was a subject the Peirces knew intimately.

5

Slavery and the Civil War along Rock Creek

IN THE YEARS BEFORE THE CIVIL WAR, the Peirce farm became known as the Peirce plantation. If the term "plantation" seems out of place in Washington, D.C., it was close to the truth in one important sense. The Peirces used slave labor for at least five decades. Collectively, the Peirce-Shoemaker family had one of largest slave-holdings in Washington in 1862, when the government freed people held in bondage in the federal city.

The migration of the Peirces and Shoemakers to Washington—and their adoption of a slave-based labor system—occurred as their Quaker brethren were nearing the climax of a great debate over the morality of slavery. For most of the eighteenth century, Friends' meetings in Pennsylvania took small but steady steps against the practice: first, discouraging members from buying newly enslaved Africans and West Indians; then, urging other Quakers to free the enslaved people they did own. By 1780, the Quakers in Pennsylvania's Chester County (the ancestral home of the Peirces and Clouds) had persuaded most members either to free their enslaved African Americans or to endure being disowned by the meeting.[1] Isaac Peirce, however, had already been disowned for marrying the daughter of another disowned Quaker (Abner Cloud Sr., ejected for fighting in the Revolution); thus, when Isaac and Abner Cloud Jr. arrived in Washington, Quaker strictures against slave-holding did not affect them.

At the time of his death in 1812, Abner Cloud Jr. held six enslaved people; they were sold as part of the court-ordered plan to pay off his debts. According to the census of 1800, Isaac Peirce held no enslaved African Americans, but by 1820, he held eleven individuals. Between 1830 and 1850, Joshua Peirce owned anywhere from six to thirteen slaves at Linnaean Hill. From 1820 until 1860, the total number of slaves in the District actually dropped by half, due in part to a decline in agricultural production and to greater demand in the Deep South, with its labor-based cotton economy. Nevertheless, during this period the Peirces' slave-holdings remained constant or grew. Interestingly, the two brothers born in 1812 and 1814 to an African-American family held in bondage on Isaac's farm had their names written in the Peirce family Bible, no less prominently than those of the Peirce children. Did Isaac Peirce father those boys? That is unknown, but the inscriptions suggest a close relationship between the Peirces and some of the African Americans they held.[2]

Although somewhat insulated by their location in rural Washington County, the Peirces belonged to a community deeply enmeshed in the institution of slavery. The capital did more commerce in the slave trade than any other American urban center, because of its location at the North-South border and good transportation links by water and by land. In Washington, free blacks (who in 1860 outnumbered enslaved African Americans in the District four to one), stood in danger of being forced back into bondage if they could not prove their status. Free or enslaved, blacks had to be off the city's streets by 10:00 p.m.

The fact that the capital of the nation dedicated to liberty for all allowed trade in human beings—coffles were driven in chains through the streets within sight of the U.S. Capitol—provoked strong abolitionist agitation in Washington. A local antislavery newspaper was published, and many attempts to free slaves were made. In 1848, hostile whites rioted in the aftermath of the failed "Pearl" plot to liberate a group of slaves via the Potomac River. A local broadside printed during this period challenged Americans to "declare in a voice of thunder, that they will not endure to have their own metropolis profaned with slavery."

In Congress, politicians repeatedly debated the merits of outlawing slavery in the District, generating intense counter-lobbying by Washington slaveholders and their sympathizers. In February 1839, a petition signed by more than two hundred Washingtonians demanded that Congress give "just respect due to the legal rights" of slaveholders, and wait for the District's own legislative council to decide the matter.* Among the signers was Pierce Shoemaker, the twenty-three-year-old grandson of Isaac Peirce.[3]

As the slavery debate grew more intense, escapes became commonplace in the District and elsewhere, especially by individuals trying to rejoin their families. Only weeks before the petition by Shoemaker and others was published, the *National Intelligencer* carried a notice offering a $150 reward for the return of a "negro man, Ned Rhodes, about 27 years old" owned by Joshua Peirce. The notice said Rhodes had been held by Peirce for a decade, adding, "he has a mother and brother living in Baltimore." Six weeks later, the newspaper reported that Rhodes' corpse had been found in a Washington canal, where he apparently had drowned. Abner Cloud, too, had at least one runaway.[4]

In 1842, Joshua Peirce offered a $50 reward for the capture of a runaway named John Chew. "John is something of a carpenter, and has been used to the culture and care of exotic plants, gardening, etc., and will probably seek such employment," Peirce's notice read.[5]

*In 1850, Congress did take the small step of banning slave trading in the District, which simply transferred the business to dealers in northern Virginia and Maryland.

Pierce Shoemaker's drawing from 1880 of an African-American woman.
Courtesy National Park Service.

Enslaved people could go to court in the District with claims that they were being held unjustly under laws governing the practice of bondage. In 1845, Andrew Jones, still a boy, was sold to Joshua Peirce on the condition that he be set free in 1857. In 1852, Jones petitioned the District Court, explaining that his mother was free and that he had been born free. Jones was represented by Daniel Ratcliffe, a Washington attorney who had been involved in the defense of the planners of the failed "Pearl" slave escape. A jury awarded Jones his freedom. Records also show that Peirce freed a slave named Clement Becket in 1838, fulfilling the conditions under which Beckett was sold to Peirce.[6]

A few Quakers living in Washington were among the most fervent antislavery campaigners, and some provided means of escape through the Underground Railroad. Beyond these individuals' ad hoc actions, was Washington's organized Quaker community involved to any extent? No evidence has been found showing that the Peirces' Quaker cousins, the Shoemakers, had a role in the escape movement. David Shoemaker Sr. is listed in the 1820 census as holding one enslaved female. His nephew, George Shoemaker, the prosperous Georgetown flour inspector and member of the Washington Quaker meeting on Eye Street, reported a "Negro runaway" in 1842.[7]

The city's Quaker meeting, though small in number, included influential figures such as Henry Clay and John Quincy Adams. In the mid-1820s, the meeting was addressed by a young English Quaker, Thomas Wetherald, known for his powerful sermons. In one discourse,

Wetherald scorned the United States as the "land of boasted liberty," where "love of money" had produced an un-Christian culture. He compared the "cruel, slave-holding oppressor" to the "whoremonger, the liar, the thief and the deceiver."[8] In 1806, slavery had been abolished in Great Britain and its colonies.

Despite strong abolitionist activity in the capital, it was dangerous, given the emotions around the issue, for Washingtonians to stand publicly against slavery. Behind closed doors, it must have been a subject discussed by the extended Peirce-Shoemaker family. The Peirces expanded their connections in the District's slave-holding subculture when, in 1855, Peirce Shoemaker married Martha Carbery, niece of the city's slave-holding former mayor, Thomas Carbery. Meanwhile, a granddaughter of Isaac Peirce married into the Ould family of Georgetown. The Ould clan included an ardent Southern sympathizer, who eventually became a ranking official in the Confederate government.[9]

With Abraham Lincoln's election in November 1860, and the spiral into war over the winter and spring, Washington was a bitterly divided city. Street fighting and barroom violence were common, angry speeches could be heard frequently in Congress, and political conspiracies were plotted in hotel rooms and private homes. Some pro-Confederate militants—such as Peirce cousin Robert Ould Jr.—packed up and moved South to join the rebellion. Virginia native William Selden, a former U.S. treasurer who lived across Rock Creek from the Peirce estate, abandoned the large house he built on seventy-three acres of land in what is now Mount Pleasant. A Southern sympathizer, Selden "was forced to sell his property at a very low price" in 1862, and return to Virginia, according to a history of the community.[10]

At the start of the war, the capital was a relatively small and—outside the federal enclave—mostly ramshackle town. Soon, more poorly built housing went up to accommodate unplanned growth, as thousands of soldiers moved though the District on their way to the war front in Virginia, or stayed in the capital waiting for orders. Escaped and later emancipated slaves from Southern states sought refuge in Washington. Meanwhile, arms and supply merchants, job-seeking opportunists, and other wartime characters swarmed into the city, which doubled in population from 1861 to 1863. Several hospitals were constructed in what would become Mount Pleasant, just across Rock Creek on the hill opposite Peirce Mill. Defensive forts were hastily erected between the Peirce-Shoemaker properties and Maryland. The closest—Fort Pennsylvania—was less than two miles from the mill.

Congress freed District slaves in 1862, after southern Democratic lawmakers left for the Confederacy, giving Republicans a majority. In a concession to local slaveholders, the law included a proviso that owners could seek compensation (non-Washingtonian slaveholders did not receive that favor in the general Emancipation of 1863). Each slaveholder was to petition the government, swearing allegiance to the Union while making a claim for

FIFTY DOLLARS REWARD.—Ran away from the subscriber, on the night of the 8th inst., negro man **JOHN**, who calls himself John Chew, sometimes John Fitzhugh. John is about five feet seven to eight inches high, stout and strong in his person, of very black color, but pleasant countenance. John is something of a carpenter, and has been used to the culture and care of exotic plants, gardening, &c. and will probably seek such employment.

I will give the above reward for his apprehension, or for such information as will enable me to secure him.
                                        JOSHUA PEIRCE,
                                        Near Washington, D. C.

Joshua Peirce offers a reward for the capture of an escaped enslaved person, 1842.
Courtesy Library of Congress.

compensation for the loss of each slave. The record shows that the Peirce and Shoemaker slave-holdings were among the capital's largest, totaling thirty-two men, women, and children. An Anacostia farmer, George Washington Young, held sixty-nine enslaved people, the largest number within Washington County.

Joshua Peirce, in his petition for compensation, described William H. Beckett as a "foreman in my garden, greenhouse, and nursery . . . familiar with various branches of that [gardening] business." Beckett could "read and write well" and was a "good coach man." Beckett also had been employed for a time by Lincoln's secretary of state, William Henry Seward. Peirce rated Jeremiah Gibson "a good salesman at the market when selling the produce off my farm and nursery." Anne Marie Rustin was an "excellent house worker" who did the cooking, washing, ironing, and sewing. Thomas Rhodes—his relation to the late Ned Rhodes, who escaped from bondage at Linnaean Hill, is unclear—was "well skilled in the management of horses . . . [an] excellent farm hand, honest, obedient, faithful, and good natured."[11]

To obtain larger payments, Washington slaveholders were known to inflate descriptions of enslaved workers, but Joshua Peirce seems genuinely to have appreciated the skills and devotion of the eleven African Americans he held in bondage. He received nearly $4,800 in total compensation from the federal government. In his will, revised in 1867, Peirce gave $2,700 to nine formerly enslaved people, in amounts ranging from $300 to $1,000, also providing for yearly payments, until death, of $48, to two others. It was a fairly generous bequest—$48 being close in $700 in 2007 inflation-adjusted dollars.

Scant information is available on the fates of the Peirce and Shoemaker slaves once they were freed. A list of workers at Linnaean Hill from 1869 showed no names of Peirce slave families, though William Beckett had returned as nursery manager, at Peirce's request. Anne Marie Rustin, by the late 1860s, was living in Rhode Island.

Aftermath of battle at Fort Stevens, July 1864.
Courtesy Library of Congress Prints and Photographs Division.

During the war Pierce Shoemaker's unmarried brother, Abner Shoemaker, lived in Washington County at his farm on Seventh Street (now Georgia Avenue), the main road north out of the city. Abner's property was about half a mile north of Fort Stevens, which guarded that approach to the capital. Abner also provided a home and cared for his elderly mother, Abigail, whose husband, government clerk David Shoemaker Jr., had died in 1850. Abigail owned property—which she leased to a man who operated a roadhouse—on the west side of Seventh Street at Rock Creek Ford Road, literally under the southern wing of the fort. Seventh Street had been improved before the war with pavement in the form of tree trunks, sawn in two lengthwise and placed flat side up to form a surface for wagons and horses. Known as the Plank Road, it was an improvement that was particularly welcome during rainy periods.

We do not know what Abner and Abigail thought of the Confederate rebellion, but relations between Fort Stevens' garrison and local residents, even Southern sympathizers, did not improve when Federal engineers deforested the area, confiscated construction materials, and destroyed homes and farm outbuildings. The residents saw their orchards felled to create clear sight lines for Union gunners. Streams were used for washing, latrines, and other functions of a rustic campsite.

Abner and Abigail had the bad luck to be living in the center of the Confederate attack on Washington in July 1864. Gen. Jubal Early led a large force across the Potomac and circled east toward Montgomery County and the city boundary. The Confederate plan was to inflict as much damage on the capital as possible, weakening the Union Army's move against Richmond.

On July 11, Confederate sharpshooters advanced past Abner Shoemaker's farm, heading directly toward the fort. They occupied vacant houses or hid behind such cover as they could find. Two large rebel units moved around the east side of the farm and headed south on a path parallel to Seventh Street.

To defend the capital, the government had mobilized thousands of troops, many of them veterans of Antietam and Gettysburg. They were supported by dozens of huge artillery pieces in Fort Stevens and nearby installations. Soldiers on both sides were emotionally charged—rebels keen to penetrate Washington's last defenses, and Federals knowing they were all that stood between the enemy and the White House. To rally his troops, President Lincoln came to the fort to watch the battle.

In a day and night of fighting, Union forces prevailed, though at high cost. One brigade lost all its regimental commanders and more than a quarter of its one thousand men, while Confederate casualties were estimated at two hundred. As the Confederates retreated north toward the Maryland line, they looted, taking livestock, stored foods, clothing, and anything else not nailed down. Adding to the destruction, Federal troops proceeded to burn down the residences and further ravage any site that might offer the Confederates cover should they return.

If the Shoemakers and their neighbors saw the battlefield afterwards (presumably they fled to their family home on Rock Creek before the fighting started), they looked on unimaginable carnage. "On all the floors [of the civilian homes], on the roofs, in the yards, within reach of the heat, were many bodies of the dead and dying, who could not be moved, and had been left behind by their [rebel] comrades," an onlooker reported, adding that "the odor of burning flesh filled air . . . a sickening spectacle." Abner Shoemaker's home was destroyed, along with the summer home of his cousin and neighbor, former Washington mayor Thomas Carbery.[12]

The mill on Rock Creek, the Peirce homestead and farm, and the Linnaean Hill nursery were insulated from the violence on Seventh Street by more than two miles of countryside. No rebels made it near the valley, though the Peirces were close enough to hear the cannon fire. A number of farm families from Washington County and Maryland took refuge on the Peirce lands.[13]

In that summer of 1864, the farm and other family businesses were being run by Pierce Shoemaker, who was almost fifty years old (Abner Peirce had died in 1851). Shoemaker had been living at the Peirce plantation since at least 1850.[14] He would preside over the plantation's final expansion, and the last decades of the mill as a commercial operation.

6

The Shoemaker Land Company

FAMILY LORE HAD PIERCE SHOEMAKER educated at Georgetown College and trained as a jeweler, but neither story could be verified.[1] "Not being of robust health, he never engaged in active business, but was vigilant as to his personal affairs, which were managed with marked ability," a Shoemaker genealogical history reported.[2] Robust or not, Pierce lived to be seventy-five, and though a late starter, would father a big family. In July 1855, just shy of age forty, he married his cousin Martha Carbery, who, according to one account, was "one of the belles of the capital in its early social life." Martha's Irish Catholic family had been prominent in city affairs almost since Washington's creation. Martha, too, came late to marriage—she was about thirty-one at the time of the ceremony at Holy Trinity Catholic Church in Georgetown. Photographs of the young couple show a handsome, dark-haired man with high cheekbones, and a round-faced, attractive woman who bears some of the features, though softly feminine, of her husband. Pierce Shoemaker was baptized and converted to Catholicism two weeks before the wedding.[3] The marriage of the Peirce plantation heir to Martha Carbery represented the final severing of the family's ties to its Quaker origins, and solidified its position among the Washington elite.

Pierce Shoemaker was not an aloof gentleman farmer inclined to leave his plantation's affairs to overseers. His ledger from the 1850s shows that he personally recorded exact details of each transaction, whether the delivery of five gallons of vinegar to his mother or the weight of the hogs slaughtered each autumn. The ledger reveals that the farm in that period grew wheat (193 bushels in 1853), rye, corn, potatoes, hay, peas, and beans, and produced wool, honey, and butter. Cider and vinegar brought a steady income. Shoemaker raised some cows and pigs, probably enough to serve the family's needs, with a few available for sale.

Records from the mill have not been found; it likely remained a profitable yet small part of the family enterprise. The mill's successful operation testified to the family's business

Pierce Shoemaker and Martha Carbery Shoemaker, undated. *Photographs from private collection.*

acumen and their millers' skills. In contrast, the Columbia mill belonging to Jonathan Shoemaker, located just downstream and later owned by President John Quincy Adams, nearly bankrupted that illustrious proprietor. It ceased operating and was removed from the tax books in 1867.[4] This could have resulted from a poorly designed mill, a bad choice of millers, ill luck, or a combination of all three factors. But, as one historian has noted, "distrust of the miller was deeply embedded in European and American folkways." The continued operation of Peirce Mill throughout the nineteenth century is certainly testimony to the owners' good judgment and oversight; they ran an operation that consistently enjoyed public trust.

By 1840, milling had become Washington's dominant industry. Peirce Mill and other Rock Creek mills remained for the most part "custom" or small-scale operations, compared to the larger "merchant" businesses on the Potomac and the C & O Canal. Volume was the key to success, because the price of a barrel of wheat flour fluctuated widely. From a high of almost $12 in 1817, it dropped to between $4.50 and $8 during the Civil War.[5]

Corn was another mainstay at the mill. John Darnell, who apparently became the miller for Pierce Shoemaker in the fall of 1859, ground 2,500 bushels of corn worth $3,000 his first year on Rock Creek. In 1870, Darnell's assistant, Whiting Tennyson, was operating the mill himself, grinding corn, wheat, and rye.[6]

Pierce Shoemaker's drawing of the family farmstead, looking west from Rock Creek, ca. 1880.
Courtesy National Park Service.

By 1860, Shoemaker had increased his cultivated land from 80 to 120 acres. Hard- and softwood trees—oak, pine, chestnut, maple, and spruce—felled to clear fields, were not discarded casually. He built a sawmill, using tree trunks for lumber, posts, and rails for fencing and firewood. Merchants bought the ashes from burned waste wood and stumps to make potash, a valued commodity essential to soap making, wool scouring, and other domestic functions. Chestnut was prized for fencing because of its resistance to water rot, and with much of Washington County still in farming, wood for fencing was a commodity in demand.*

A rapidly expanding Washington needed wood for building and for heat. Shoemaker was planting new trees, showing he viewed the timber trade as a future revenue source. His ledger covering the years 1850 to 1857 reveals that in those years his timber business grew substantially, while income from farming lagged.[8]

*Chestnut wood was part of the famous debut of the telegraphic system of inventor Samuel F. B. Morse, who contracted to buy five hundred posts from Pierce Shoemaker's brother, Abner, in February 1844. In May, Morse sent his first message, "What Hath God Wrought," through wires mounted on chestnut posts along the railroad tracks between Washington and Baltimore.[9]

Lewis Carbery, undated portrait. *Courtesy Historical Society of Washington, D.C.*

ON HER FATHER'S SIDE, Martha Carbery's family immigrated to Boston from Ireland in the seventeenth century, then moved to St. Mary's County, Maryland, living there for nearly one hundred years. Thomas Carbery Sr. settled in Washington around 1800, prospering as a building supplies contractor during the capital's first wave of construction. His brother, Henry Carbery, a Revolutionary War officer, was commander of White House guard forces in August 1814, when the British burned Washington. Historians suggest that such early prominent involvement in city affairs (the creation of Georgetown College is another example) exempted the Catholic faithful in Washington from much of the raw prejudice that surfaced in New York, Boston, and elsewhere during the nineteenth century.

Thomas Carbery Jr., born in 1791, followed his father into the construction business and built a profitable wharf that received shipments to the White House and other government buildings. In 1822, he became the city's sixth (and first popularly elected) mayor. An advocate for District home rule and universal suffrage for white males, he was also leader of a growing minority, for by 1850, the Irish would become the largest ethnic group in Washington. A staunch Democrat, he has been referred to by some Washington historians as the tribune of the "Poor Man's Party." Carbery helped organize the campaign to build the Washington Monument, and for the last eight years of his life was president of what became the National Metropolitan Bank. His house and gardens stood at Seventeenth and C Streets, NW, now the site of Constitution Hall. It was at that house in 1823 that Carbery's sister, Ann Mattingly, made an unexplained recovery from cancer that Washington's Catholic community regarded as miraculous. Thomas Carbery was a substantial slaveholder, freeing twelve African Americans in the 1862 emancipation; he also donated land for St. Vincent's Orphan Asylum, built near Tenth and F Streets, NW.

In 1817, Thomas Carbery's brother, Lewis, the surveyor of Washington County and president of the Levy Court, married Artemesia Cloud, daughter of Abner Cloud Jr. The third Carbery brother, James, married Artemesia's sister Emza. It was Lewis and Artemesia Carbery's daughter, Martha, who married Pierce Shoemaker.[7]

CONSTRUCTION OF THE Chesapeake and Ohio Canal, begun in 1828, allowed merchants to inexpensively transport wheat and flour from the new western agricultural lands to the port cities of Georgetown and Alexandria, and then transship to other American ports and overseas. In 1860, nearly sixteen million barrels of American flour were exported. The C & O Canal also gave mills in Georgetown an insurmountable advantage over the Rock Creek mills. The canal delivered a consistent "head" of water up to twenty feet above the level of the Potomac River, far more than any mill dam located along Rock Creek could provide. At their peak, the eight mills along the Potomac near Georgetown, and the Lyon Mill on Rock Creek, are estimated to have produced about two thousand barrels daily.[10]

Another family artifact, a binder containing mostly undated pencil drawings signed by Pierce Shoemaker, portrays in somewhat naïve artistic terms a bucolic scene viewed from the east side of Rock Creek. Several rustic homes and outbuildings are shown, with sparse tree cover and grazing cattle. One drawing shows hounds chasing a fox through the hills. The mill itself is difficult to discern, since there is no sign of the water and wheel. There are also sketches of several unidentified persons, including one dated 1880 of an African-American woman who may have been a servant at the plantation.[11]

Emancipation of slaves in the District meant that Peirce Plantation and other farms would need to adjust their operations to account for increased labor costs. It is unknown whether any of Pierce Shoemaker's former slaves stayed with him as hired hands after emancipation (a Linnaean Hill payroll list dating to the late 1860s shows no names of individuals enslaved by Joshua Peirce). In any event, by 1870, Shoemaker had reduced his cultivated land to 100 acres; at that time, he owned a total of 608 acres, valued at $83,000. Abner Peirce's holdings, which Pierce Shoemaker inherited, totaled 960 acres, according to the 1850 census, so Shoemaker may have sold or given away to other family members the difference between these two figures.

The family landholdings extended into Virginia and demonstrate that the Peirces and Shoemakers expanded their commercial interests in land and real estate even before Washington's construction and population boom that began during the Civil War. In April 1848, Abner Peirce advertised for sale "several hundred acres of land" between Rockville Turnpike and Rock Creek; two years earlier he had offered what seemed to be similar land "with several valuable mill-seats."[12]

In 1850, a year before his death, Abner Peirce paid $4,000 for just under 300 acres of land in Fairfax County, near the Loudoun County line and present-day site of Dulles

International Airport. The 1860 census shows the land being farmed, with the usual complement of animals, including sheep, cattle, and hogs.[13]

The family also owned land in the McLean area of Fairfax. In 1877, Pierce Shoemaker sold about five acres to a Hiram Kinner and his wife, farmers living in the Lincolnville community of former slaves. The terms specified only that the Kinners put down $16, paying the balance at 8 percent interest over five years. These were "not unreasonable terms considering the scarcity of money" in the hardscrabble area after the Civil War, a study suggested.[14]

The 1870s were a boom time for milling, as operators paid the Shoemakers between $1,200 and $1,500 in annual rent. "It was a daily occurrence to see from ten to twelve teams and a number of boys on horseback from the surrounding country with grist," recalled one of Pierce Shoemaker's sons. "Grain could be hauled to the mills of Rock Creek from Georgetown, made into flour, and sold on the Washington market at a profit."[15]

Pierce and Martha Shoemaker had seven children, born in rapid succession between 1856 and 1864. Martha died before her forty-third birthday, two years after the birth of their final child. Three children died in their teens or twenties. Pierce Shoemaker did not remarry, but in the mid-1870s, he decided to build a new house to replace the crowded family cottage. Up the hill from Rock Creek, the new home, called "Cloverdale" like the family's previous house, was flanked by the existing stone springhouse, a carriage house, and a distillery. Pierce's unknown architect employed an unusual cross-gambrel style for the house, with a mansard roof fashionable during that period. Its wide, covered front porch looked down on Rock Creek and the mill.

Shoemaker's decision to build Cloverdale is significant, coming as it did near the end of the administration of President Ulysses S. Grant, a time of unprecedented corruption in Washington and the beginning of a thirty-year influx into the capital of rich and powerful status-seekers and would-be influence peddlers. One way newcomers made their mark was by erecting grand mansions for living and entertaining during Washington's social season. Cloverdale, though handsome, was neither gaudy nor excessive compared to some of the homes rising around Pacific (later Dupont) Circle in that period. The Peirces and Shoemakers, with their growing wealth, joined other "old families" of Washington (a relative term, of course, since most had lived there for less than a century, unlike venerable clans in Philadelphia, New York, and Boston) in delineating their own world of refined taste and decorum.

Thus, Joshua Peirce, two years before his death in 1869, became one of the initial members of the Association of Oldest Inhabitants of the District of Columbia. The group formed in 1865 as the city's "Antiques" saw that the Civil War and its tumult had upended the city, imperiling their position in its hierarchy. As Kathryn Allamong Jacob described it in her account of Washington's nineteenth-century high society:

> During the war, Washington's old families suffered a special, devastating blow more concrete and dramatic than any other city's old elite would endure. The core of the antebellum capital's old residential elite had been Southern and Democratic, with fortunes based on slaves and land in Maryland and Virginia. Their ranks were decimated by the war just as surely as the ranks of soldiers in blue and gray had been mowed down on the battlefields.[16]

For the Peirce-Shoemaker clan, however, dispossession was more symbolic than real, since Pierce Shoemaker and Joshua Peirce survived the war with their land and bank accounts intact. Nevertheless, these descendants of solid Pennsylvanian Quaker stock now regarded northern Republicans—who in the years after the Civil War dominated the national government and official Washington—as somewhat strange and distant cousins. Searching for a way to describe Pierce Shoemaker's physical appearance, a family friend once said he "bore a striking resemblance" to the Confederate Gen. Robert E. Lee, a comparison thoroughly acceptable among Washington's Southern-oriented population.[17]

Cloverdale, the Shoemaker homestead, ca. 1901.
Photograph courtesy Judith Helm.

The Washington Foundlings Hospital, created through a bequest of Joshua Peirce, ca. 1895. *Courtesy Historical Society of Washington, D.C.*

JOSHUA PEIRCE'S DECISION TO SUPPORT AN ORPHANAGE may have arisen from his experience on the Washington County Levy Court, which besides taxes and road building was responsible for relief work. His own childless marriage also may have been a factor. In any event, the Washington Home for Foundlings, as it was called, faced several obstacles that delayed the fulfillment of Peirce's bequest until nearly twenty years after his death in 1869. Pierce Shoemaker (though later a member of the public-spirited Oldest Inhabitants association), joined with other Peirce heirs to contest the donation of land for the orphanage. Shoemaker's attorney questioned the virtues of such institutions.

The case went to the U.S. Supreme Court, which rebuffed the plaintiffs with the observation that "there are no beneficiaries more needing protection, care and kindness . . . than these waifs, helpless and abandoned upon the sea of life." In addition, fundraising to build the new home took much longer than expected. It finally opened in 1887, on Fifteenth Street, NW, between R and S Streets. The institution took in more than five hundred infants and young children in its first decade, who were cared for until adoptive parents could be found. All the children were white, in keeping with the segregation in force at that time. Most were abandoned by unwed mothers, and often were in poor health. The mortality rate was about 70 percent. In 1929, the home moved to a new building in Tenleytown, where it housed young children until 1957, after which it became an adoption agency.[18]

The spendthrift habits and civic irresponsibility of the nouveaux riches and parvenus who flocked to Washington angered the Oldest Inhabitants group. The founding members declared in their constitution that, as the District's original residents, "we cherish the greatest solicitude for its welfare," and that the association would "lend its aid in every way" to support "good order" and "right government." In 1867, the year that Joshua Peirce joined the Oldest Inhabitants, he revised his will both to provide for larger cash bequests to the African Americans he once held in bondage and to donate land he owned in Washington City for a new orphanage.

Besides their good works, native Washingtonians such as Joshua Peirce usually handled their wealth in a conservative fashion. The city block adjoining the land donated for the orphanage was also owned by Peirce. In 1864, he subdivided it into ninety-five narrow lots suitable for residences.[19] Peirce was wagering that the Civil War's expansion of the city was going to be permanent.

Charity could not, however, address the lack of sewers, paved roads, and other standard amenities in Washington's urban core, which the Civil War's population boom had exacerbated. In 1871, Congress united Georgetown, Washington City, and Washington County (previously, each entity was self-governing) in hopes that a territorial form of government would improve the management and finances of the capital. Alexander Shepherd, vice chairman of the public works board and later governor, orchestrated a vigorous campaign of civic improvements that began transforming Washington into a respectable metropolis. But Shepherd's free spending quickly bankrupted the municipal treasury, and within three years the territorial system was dissolved. Congress then decided to appoint a three-person commission to run municipal affairs.

Pierce Shoemaker, as a local squire positioned in Washington's outlying countryside, was little affected by the city's turmoil. His standing is illustrated in coverage by the *Washington Post* of his two daughters' weddings. A story from November 1878, on Caroline Shoemaker's wedding to William Ketler, a San Francisco businessman, describes her father as "one of the most prominent citizens of Washington County." The wedding at "venerable Trinity church" (Holy Trinity Catholic Church in Georgetown) was "intended to be a very quiet affair, only the immediate family, relatives, and intimate friends being invited, but there were so many of these that the church was nearly half-filled, many of the oldest and most prominent citizens of Georgetown and the county being present."[20]

Eight years later, Clara Shoemaker married Edwin A. Newman, a Washington attorney, at St. Matthew's Catholic Church near the White House. The *Post* called the event a "fashionable wedding in Catholic circles," noting that the "ceremony was performed inside the chancel rail, which is a rare occurrence in the Catholic church." Normally, this special treatment was reserved for royalty. The groom and his bride, "a beautiful brunette . . . tall and graceful," honeymooned in New York City.[21]

7

Klingle's Mansion

THE DEATH OF JOSHUA PEIRCE left Linnaean Hill in the hands of his nephew and adopted son, Joshua Peirce Klingle. Born in Philadelphia in 1835, the younger man was named for his uncle. While Joshua Klingle was still a child, his mother and father died, and the childless Peirces took the orphaned boy into their home in Washington.

Joshua Klingle attended Columbian College (later George Washington University), which in those days stood about a mile and a half from Linnaean Hill, on high ground along the road to his father's nursery in town.

"The view from College Hill is surpassingly beautiful," reads a contemporary description of the institution's setting. "The student can sit in his room and cast his eye over scenes which are well calculated to arouse the sluggish, to interest the most unobservant, and to excite feelings of energy and patriotism . . . the Capitol, the President's house, and the other public buildings are within his view; the Potomac stretches away before him as far as his vision can reach."[1]

As was customary in that era, Klingle entered college as a young adolescent. He graduated in 1851, the year he turned sixteen, with a bachelor of arts degree. Afterwards he helped his uncle manage the horticultural business, later telling acquaintances that he had overseen the planting of trees from the nursery in many of Washington's parks and squares. In 1861, Klingle was named to the Levy Court of Washington County, replacing his uncle as a member of the board that oversaw road building and taxes.

During the Civil War, Klingle was of prime draft age, but he made use of a legal loophole familiar to sons of wealthy families and paid a $300 fee to escape service in the Union army. It is hard to say whether Klingle was a Southern sympathizer or simply unwilling to serve.[2] His first wife, Laura Tiernan, was from a family of the Virginia Tidewater's elite. Laura's mother, Gay Robertson Bernard, belonged to a clan prominent in Port Royal, one of the first

towns built on the Rappahannock River. Gay Bernard married Charles Tiernan, a well-to-do Baltimore merchant, and moved to that city. Evidently, during the war Gay Tiernan was active in Baltimore's pro-Confederate circles.[3]

Klingle and Laura Tiernan were married in October 1865, at the neoclassical Baltimore cathedral (today known as the Baltimore Basilica) by the city's archbishop, the country's senior Roman Catholic prelate.[4] In 1869, after Joshua Peirce's death, Klingle inherited Linnaean Hill. By that time, the nursery's city branch apparently had closed. The land was being sold for development, and an inventory of Peirce's estate showed a very limited selection of trees, shrubs, and flowers. In a letter that year, Klingle referred to the city branch in the past tense.

Klingle evidently disagreed with his uncle on management of the business, including labor arrangements at the nursery. In 1867, two years before he died, Joshua Peirce offered a large sum of money to his former slave and nursery foreman William Beckett, hoping to persuade him to return. According to a deposition, Peirce told Daniel Cleclezer, a blacksmith with whom he may have done business, that "he must get William Beckett back, that if he did not get him back, that he [Peirce] must stop his business" since it was "impossible to carry on his business without him." Peirce promised to make Beckett "easy through life" if he returned. Beckett, evidently working elsewhere in the city, did return to work for his former owner. And later that year Peirce revised his will to give Beckett two special gifts: a lump sum of $1,000 and a promissory note naming Klingle as the beneficiary, valued at $2,000.[5]

In a second deposition, Cleclezer said that Peirce had specified that "Beckett should not be interfered with by Mr. Klingle or anyone else," and that Beckett—Peirce's "bookkeeper, salesman, and gardener"—was to be paid $100 per month.

Nevertheless, after Peirce died, when Beckett requested a retroactive salary of $100 per month for his two previous years as foreman, Klingle balked. Beckett's demand was "preposterous" and "absurd," Klingle charged in a five-page letter to the estate's executors. "First class men in the best business-houses in Washington City do not unless in exceptional cases have salaries averaging more than that amount," Klingle wrote. Linnaean Hill "has been carried in at a loss for several years and particularly during the time that Beckett has charged $100 per month for acting as foreman," the new proprietor added. The manager of the city branch of the business had only received $200 per year plus a house, he said, offering to pay Beckett not $100 monthly but $20. In his letter, Klingle acknowledged that Beckett had helped nurse Peirce through his final weeks of illness, but concluded that "his pretended

Joshua Peirce Klingle, by Hector Eaches, ca. 1860.
Courtesy Colonial Dames of America, Chapter III.
Photograph by Lee Stalsworth.

affection for my Uncle was of the same character as those others White as well as Black whose affection was merely a lively sense of favors to come."

The executors asked Pierce Shoemaker, whose farm bordered Linnaean Hill, for his opinion of the Beckett dispute. In a brief letter, Shoemaker said he did not think the foreman's $100 request unreasonable, adding that from "personal observation" he believed Beckett's services to be "valuable" and "indispensable." Shoemaker's letter also bore the signature of his neighbor, Dr. Henry Holt.

Amid such conflicting perspectives, the executors—one was John Blake, president of Washington's National Metropolitan Bank—asked the District of Columbia's Supreme Court to decide the matter. No such decision can be found, but records show Beckett being paid $50 per month in a six-month period while the matter was under dispute.[6]

Within a few months of Joshua Peirce's death, Klingle evidently closed Linnaean Hill's business operation, turning his attention to other matters, such as managing his uncle's property in the city. He served on the first board of directors of the Washington Home for Foundlings, which his late uncle had created, and over time became a civic volunteer and financial policy advocate. As a well-to-do member of a respected family, Klingle was a natural recruit for the era's Populist Party movement, which thrived on opposition to the power wielded by the new elite of the Gilded Age. By the late 1870s, Klingle belonged to the District of Columbia Labor Exchange, a civic body formed to deal with unemployment.

In January 1880, Klingle appeared at a rally espousing home rule for the District. Newspaper ads promoting the meeting castigated the debt-ridden "despotic appointive government over us," and claimed that "500 of our best citizens are houseless and homeless today in consequence of excessive taxation." A few months later, in a letter printed in the *Washington Post,* Klingle fulminated against his fellow citizens' waste of water, arguing that the city should meter water use. In subsequent statistics-laden contributions to the newspaper's letter column, Klingle proposed new financial policies for the District government that he contended would provide more money for street improvements.[7]

Klingle avidly endorsed continued governmental use of silver and gold to fix the value of a monetary unit.* His advocacy of "bimetallism," as it was known, was part of an emotional populist campaign against the rule of gold that culminated in Democrat William Jennings Bryan's presidential campaign in 1896. In that era, Klingle and the Shoemakers were decidedly Democratic in their partisan allegiance—that is, they were Southern Democrats, for the capital's local political culture, after the brief period of radical reconstruction, had reverted to historical form. In 1880, nearly 80 percent of Washington's 101,000 whites had been born in the District, or in some southern state. Washington's large African-American

---

*In 1873, Congress demonetized silver, triggering deflation that hurt farmers and others who did not see the change coming; coincidentally, it also led to an export of more grain to Europe where prices were higher.

community was disenfranchised, relegated to pseudo-citizenship. In Frederick Douglass's view, antebellum Washington was "southern in all its sympathies and national only in name." After the war, it could be argued, the same applied. Many wealthy Northerners would make the capital their home, but by the late nineteenth century, the city's homegrown elite was redoubling efforts to make Washington a southern business capital, with the attendant segregation and economic oppression.

Klingle's prominence as a civic activist and the well-to-do son of Joshua Peirce brought unwelcome attention on an embarrassing series of events involving the family's only child. Beatrice Klingle was raised at Linnaean Hill and educated at the Academy of the Visitation, a Catholic girl's school on lower Connecticut Avenue.[8] "The deep love and pride of Mr. and Mrs. Klingle were centered on their daughter," Harry Shannon, the *Evening Star's* "Rambler" columnist later wrote. "She was a beautiful child who grew into a charming woman," Shannon recalled. "Where Klingle Lane forded Rock Creek and where the fallen oak formed a foot bridge . . . Beatrice had a rustic bench, and there on the gorgeous afternoons of summer she would sit and read. She seemed to love the spot even when she was a little girl."[9]

Upon graduating from the Academy of the Visitation in June 1883, Beatrice emerged as one of Washington society's most courted debutantes. Two years later, at age 18, she eloped with Edward I. Darling, a promising young composer and the son of New York writer Flora Adams Darling, a founder of the Daughters of the American Revolution.

The late 1800s saw American newspapers on the verge of becoming a mass-market industry, catering to a popular appetite for sensation, including scandals involving upper-crust families. The Klingle affair received front-page coverage in the *Post,* in September 1885, and the *Star* and other newspapers followed with stories on Klingle's frantic and unsuccessful search for Beatrice, and her move to New York City. Two months later, Klingle suffered another blow when his wife, Laura, died at the age of forty-one, of what records term "abdominal fever."

Beatrice Klingle's short life ended in confused and gothic circumstances. She died in 1895, not yet thirty, at a California health resort, diagnosed as suffering from "nervous prostration, caused by the cruel slanders of a vindictive person," her attorney told reporters. That allegedly "vindictive person" was her mother-in-law, Flora Adams Darling, who a few weeks earlier had accused Beatrice of poisoning her son so she could marry another man. Though never proven, that charge, too, was covered by the Washington press, and the *New York Times.*[10]

Klingle had died three years before this final sad chapter in his daughter's life. When he succumbed to an apparent heart attack, on July 4, 1892, he was living with his second wife in a townhouse on S Street, NW, around the corner from the Washington Home for Foundlings, on land that once had been the city branch of the Linnaean Hill nursery. Subdivided into narrow lots, the Pierce properties rapidly were filling with brick and frame homes.*

Pierce Shoemaker had died the previous year. At the time of his death, business at the mill was slowing to a trickle. Less land was being cultivated in Washington, and commercial flour could be shipped in cheaply from Baltimore, Philadelphia, and other cities. The national focus of grain production had shifted to the Midwest, where massive quantities could be grown and milled at lower prices. By 1880, Peirce Mill seems mainly to have been producing feed for animals; its flour production for the year was only ten barrels. The traditional wooden waterwheel was gone, having been replaced in the mid-1870s by a metal turbine that could generate greater waterpower. But by 1890, brothers Alcibiades and Charles White, who operated the mill, were paying Pierce Shoemaker a mere $20 a month, only a fifth of what had been paid two decades earlier.[11]

In the final decades of the nineteenth century, Peirce Mill was a popular destination point for Washingtonians of all backgrounds. President Grover Cleveland rode in his carriage from the White House to the mill on Independence Day 1885, returning by way of the Tennallytown road (today's Wisconsin Avenue). "The President's equipage was recognized by a number of picnic parties, and he was kept busy responding to salutations until the last hill was climbed," the *Post* reported. Horsemen of the Chevy Chase hunt used Peirce Mill as a starting point for a northward "run of the hounds," and bicyclists made the stone building a landmark for their outings.[12]

In recognition of the great enjoyment the Rock Creek valley brought to citizens, efforts were underway by the federal government to turn much of the Shoemaker family's holdings into America's first urban park. Representing the clan in what proved to be a contentious transfer of property was Pierce Shoemaker's eldest son, Louis Pierce Shoemaker.

*For many years, the Klingle name labeled a ford across Rock Creek southwest of the Linnaean Hill house. Today, the name is given to a road that runs intermittently through northwest Washington, D.C., and until the early 1990s, down a steep hill to Rock Creek Park. The tributary alongside the road bears the Klingle name, as does the bridge carrying the road across the creek. Joshua Klingle's Linnaean Hill home (the house built by Joshua Peirce) is known as Klingle Mansion and is the headquarters for the Rock Creek Park staff.

8

"The Celebrated Rock Creek Park Case"

BORN FIVE YEARS BEFORE THE CIVIL WAR ERUPTED, Louis Shoemaker grew up at the old Peirce homestead overlooking Rock Creek. Though he lost his mother, Martha Carbery Shoemaker, at the age of ten, he had the consolation of a large family, including three younger brothers with whom to play in the nearby forests and streams. As they grew, Pierce Shoemaker's sons likely worked or did chores on the prosperous plantation; in childhood and as teenagers they certainly had front row seats at their family's busy country mill. Besides the daily arrival of numerous horse-drawn wagons filled with grist, Louis Shoemaker had warm memories of the "magnificent trees, the rugged and picturesque character of the landscape [and] the great number of huge rocks deposited" in Rock Creek. Trees, he once said, were his "best friends."[1]

Louis Shoemaker was not destined to take over the estate, however. In keeping with his family's pattern of steady upward mobility, he was sent to parochial school at St. Patrick's Catholic Church on Tenth Street, NW.* Louis later attended Georgetown University, earning a law degree in 1881. Already involved in the land and development business, he opened an office in 1876, on F Street, near Ninth Street, NW, around the corner from the St. Patrick's school, and in the commercial center of the Washington real estate world. His career choice fit what was becoming the accepted wisdom of how entrepreneurs in Washington would create wealth: not through "bricks and mortar" industry, but through real estate development, construction, and finance, ideally suited to meet the unique needs of the capital.

Shoemaker came of age as Alexander Shepherd, the ambitious first and only territorial governor, was commanding a full-scale modernization of the capital. Georgetown, Washington City, and Washington County had just been united under a single municipal administration, forming the area north of the Potomac that is enclosed by today's District

*The school was later renamed St. John's College High School. Today it is located on Military Road near the entrance to Rock Creek Park.

The storefront of Louis Shoemaker's real estate firm, at 920 F Street, NW, in 1895. *Courtesy Historical Society of Washington, D.C.*

boundary. To house clerks and other bureaucrats, to board lobbyists, and to accommodate tourists, Washington would need apartments, single-family homes, and hotels. Retail facilities and transportation infrastructure, plus power and communications services, had to be constructed and constantly updated. In 1887 alone, nearly 2,500 buildings were raised in the capital; in the previous five years, land prices in desirable areas had jumped from eight to forty-eight cents a square foot.[2]

In the 1860s, pollution at the back doorstep of the White House, which then fronted on the sewage-filled Washington Canal, prompted suggestions for a new presidential residence on higher ground, perhaps in the vicinity of Rock Creek. Some in Congress went further, arguing to move the capital city to the Midwest. That latter notion had faded by the 1880s, but a national movement for large public recreational spaces within major cities (such as New York's Central Park) had taken hold. A campaign for a major park in Washington sprang up, supported by the leaders of major banks, other business executives, and politicians. The leaders also included the owner of the *Evening Star,* Crosby Noyes, who used his newspaper to publicize the effort. After many years of congressional debate, in September 1890, President Benjamin Harrison signed into law a measure appropriating $1.2 million to purchase a maximum of two thousand acres along both sides of Rock Creek.

At that time, the Shoemaker family and Joshua Klingle owned anywhere from six hundred to seven hundred acres spread out in large and small plots between Military Road and Piney Branch—the heart of the property targeted for the park. Not all the family's land would be selected, since some of it extended well beyond the creek. Yet, if patterns of real estate speculation in other cities applied to Washington, then the land adjacent to the proposed park would gain value. This theory allowed the Shoemakers and Klingle to argue for a high appraisal of their property.

Earlier, in 1889, Louis Shoemaker, seasoned in real estate brokerage, hinted at his negotiating position when the federal government talked to Rock Creek landowners about buying some one hundred acres for the future National Zoo, just south of Linnaean Hill. Shoemaker told a reporter, "I would prefer that they select a portion along the northern end of the [Shoemaker-owned] tract . . . where I think the country is admirably suited for the purpose, but still if they prefer the southern terminus of the tract I shall be glad to treat with them."[3]

Shoemaker may have thought he would get a better price from private buyers for the southern acreage, or he may have had other ideas. But his gentlemanly comments masked deep concern about the proposed parkland purchase. The congressional appropriation allowed an average maximum of $600 per acre, although a plot with existing improvements could command a better price. With residential Washington rapidly expanding north from the city core, appraisals of land adjoining Rock Creek put its open market value at $1,000 to $2,000 per acre.

By March 1891, the Rock Creek Park Commission appointed by Congress to buy the land had finished its assessments, including what to offer Shoemaker and others. "Will these offers be accepted?" the *Star* asked. "One is pretty safe in saying that they will not. . . nobody thinks that it can be done without going to law about it."

The commission held two days of meetings in the War Department to hear property owners' responses to the proffered prices. Joshua Klingle accepted their offer of $2,000 per acre for thirty-two acres, which reflected the value of the Linnaean Hill estate, but there is no record of Shoemaker meeting the commissioners. Instead, he organized a meeting of fellow Rock Creek landowners with his personal attorney, Tallmadge Lambert, at which the group vowed not to accept the prices offered by the government.

Lambert, like Shoemaker, was a Georgetown College graduate and member of the city's legal and financial elite. During his career—cut short by a stroke in his mid-fifties—Lambert was a director of the Washington Board of Trade, treasurer of the Union Savings Bank, and came close to being appointed a District judge. He was also president of the Great Falls Ice Company, and was once accused by a Washington dairy of conspiring with other frozen water vendors of engineering an "ice trust."[4]

Within a few weeks of the meeting at Lambert's office, Shoemaker and other property owners arranged to have the trees felled on land designated for the park. In late May, a District judge issued an injunction against Shoemaker and the others for defacing the new parkland. Arguments by Shoemaker's lawyer, the judge said, "are practically admissions that [Shoemaker] has been, according to his own taste and discretion cutting such trees as he saw fit to cut with a view to rendering the rest of his lands more valuable, and this, the court thinks, he has no right to do under the circumstances."[5]

The federal government had made it clear that it would condemn the land and take the acreage by right of eminent domain. In a ruling that summer, the D.C. Supreme Court repudiated Shoemaker's claim against appropriation of private land for a public park. Shoemaker's attorney argued that parks were not an example of "public use" in a constitutional sense; the judge voiced confidence that the government knew what it was doing (besides, it was compensating the owners). If further justification was needed, authorities had the right to seize the entire Rock Creek area—"to prevent its waters from being polluted by the offal of slaughterhouses and of disgusting factories" that are "bringing their abominations into the midst of the city to poison and infect the air," the judge wrote, reflecting the era's progressive view about conservation and public health issues.[6]

The Rock Creek Park Commission, meanwhile, had been unable to come to terms with most of the landowners, and assigned the matter to a court-appointed appraisal body. That committee set a figure that exceeded the congressional appropriation by $230,000. This forced the commission to reduce its acquisition by about 300 acres. Instead of 1,900 acres, Rock Creek Park would comprise a little more than 1,600 acres. The appraisers allowed $314,000 for the Shoemaker estate's 350 acres.[7] That came out to less than $1,000 an acre, compared to the maximum of $1,500 the owners had considered fair value for their various holdings.

Shoemaker fought the matter all the way to the U.S. Supreme Court, meanwhile enlisting his brother-in-law, attorney Edwin A. Newman, in a corollary public relations campaign. "Now don't think I don't like parks and public improvements; I do," Newman wrote to the *Post,* asking whether the full cost of the park and its maintenance had been considered. "But we ought not to buy more than we can pay for conveniently."[8]

At the Supreme Court, Shoemaker's lawyers challenged park commission actions on procedural and constitutional grounds, and also claimed that Shoemaker's holdings were worth more, because they might have gold deposits. The justices heard the arguments during two days in late November 1892. "Quite an array of legal talent appeared at the bar," a *Post* reporter wrote, calling it the "celebrated Rock Creek Park case."

The U.S. attorneys observed that the right of eminent domain is "essential" to the government's "independent existence and perpetuity" and had to outrank the "obstinacy of a private person." As for gold, no appreciable amount of precious metal had been found on Shoemaker's land, and even if it had, the attorneys noted, the government owned mineral rights in Washington, since it was a federal district.[9]

The Supreme Court ruled two months later. Associate Justice George Shiras wrote the unanimous opinion upholding every lower court opinion. Despite the defeat, Shoemaker remained dissatisfied with the government's mandate and tactics. He continued to contest the issue in public for several years, calling the federal law establishing the park "obnoxious" and suggesting the government was "trifling" with a thousand years of Anglo-Saxon precedent in property rights. Legal issues and self-interest aside, Shoemaker did make a valid point about the acquisition's financing: District taxpayers had to pay half the price of a park clearly designated as a national treasure to benefit all citizens.[10]

Louis Pierce Shoemaker, ca. 1915. *Courtesy Historical Society of Washington, D.C.*

PHOTOGRAPHS OF LOUIS P. SHOEMAKER are remarkably similar: a stern-looking man with bald pate and neatly trimmed beard. He lived at Cloverdale until his marriage to Kathryn Gallagher, an Augusta, Georgia, native, whom he met while she was attending a Catholic boarding school in Baltimore. Married when she was eighteen, and he in his late twenties, they moved to the District's Brightwood area, east of Rock Creek Park, where the Shoemakers owned land that was still largely rural. There, on a twenty-acre lot bordered by today's Georgia Avenue, Shoemaker built his "Oak Grove" estate. It was elaborately landscaped, and featured a large pond formed by the damming of a Rock Creek tributary. Further north, at the Maryland state line, Shoemaker's sister, Abigail, and her husband, Charles R. Newman, constructed a home on land also owned by the family (today, the modified house is known as the Blair Mansion Inn).

Brightwood was the setting for a good deal of Shoemaker's real estate activities, as he focused on developing new communities at Washington's outskirts. Working around the Washington Board of Trade, whose members lobbied for development of the land they owned west of Rock Creek, Shoemaker argued strenuously for the extension of streetcar lines and other city services to his neighborhood. As president of the Brightwood Citizens Association for more than a decade (1900 to 1916), he persuaded key members of Congress to locate the Walter Reed U.S. Military Hospital in the community in 1908.[11]

This era of Washington history was one of turbo-charged real estate speculation, and muckrakers had a field day linking prominent members of Congress and some D.C. commissioners to insider trading and payoffs. Though he was in the thick of this tainted world, Shoemaker's name does not appear in the journalistic narratives exposing the period's dark side. The record does document his status as a key financial player (board memberships including the Washington Loan and Trust Co., the Potomac Insurance Co., and the Columbia National Bank), and vigorous civic booster (involvement with the Meridian Hills and Lanier Heights citizens groups; founder and president of the Takoma Park Club; and donor of sixteen hundred books to the core collection of the Takoma Park, D.C., library that opened in 1911).[12]

Some aspects of Shoemaker's personal life strangely echoed those of Joshua Klingle's. Both men had only one child, and both offspring were involved in marriages sensationalized by the local press. In Shoemaker's case, it was his son's marriage to a wealthy woman more than twice his age (following a reported romance with the woman's daughter). A little more than a year after that episode, Shoemaker's wife died of a heart ailment at age forty-five. Katie Shoemaker, as she was known, was memorialized in one obituary as "one of Washington's best known philanthropists and charity workers." Her funeral service was "attended by more than 1,000 persons," and many who were in attendance "had received her assistance in an hour of need." Louis Shoemaker later married Harriet Simms, a member of an old and prominent District family.[13]

Shoemaker's long battle against the federal government may have been over principle and his lost family heritage, and was certainly over money, but the outcome was never a threat to his personal wealth and prominence. Eventually, Shoemaker swallowed his pride and became a major advocate for development of public facilities in the park, including preservation of Peirce Mill.

Shoemaker had a "strong forceful character" and was "vigorous in debate, and at all times in thorough command of himself," family friend John A. Saul said in a personal recollection. Yet, Shoemaker also was an able conciliator: "Many are the occasions when storms appeared to be brewing, he smoothed and harmonized conflicting parties by his skill and good nature." Shoemaker's civic spirit, Saul said, reflected his family's record of local government service. "It came by right from both sides of the house."[14]

Politically, Shoemaker remained in the family's conservative, Southern Democratic tradition, possessing a more pronounced pro-business attitude than his cousin, Joshua Klingle. Shoemaker took a dim view of unions, increased government regulation, and taxes. Yet Shoemaker demonstrated his devotion to the Union by handling the arrangements for Memorial Day encampments by veterans of the Grand Army of the Republic. He also led ceremonies, a few blocks from his home, at the Fort Stevens cemetery commemorating the defense of Washington during the Civil War. Continuing to write and speak on District affairs, Shoemaker endorsed home rule, and joined a delegation that met with President Woodrow Wilson to advocate that perennially hopeless cause. Putting aside whatever suspicions he held about Wilson's progressive tendencies, Shoemaker, as a delegate to the 1916 Democratic convention in St. Louis, backed the president for a second term.

Though Peirce Mill and much of the surrounding land officially were incorporated into Rock Creek Park in 1892, the government allowed the mill operation to continue, probably more out of charity than anything else. But in 1897, the turbine machinery failed. "I was grinding a load of rye for a neighbor when the main shaft of the mill broke," miller Alcibiades White recalled. "I was about half through, and the neighbor had to haul his unground rye away, and I guess he never got it ground."[15] The collapse put an end to a mill operation that had begun to wither many years earlier.

Beginning in 1895, administration of the park lay with a board representing the commissioners of the District of Columbia and including the chief of engineers for the U.S. Army. The board authorized a gradual improvement of roads and bridges throughout the park, and other facilities. The pace was too slow for Shoemaker and his fellow Brightwood residents who lived east of Rock Creek Park's northern edge. Late in the summer of 1903,

Shoemaker opened a public campaign for more vigorous improvements. "Long ago," he wrote to the *Evening Star*, the park "ought to have been made accessible to our people by the judicious construction of driveways, bridges, footways, bridal paths and closely approximating electric car lines." He called on the federal government to fund "tennis, golf, croquet, and ball grounds, encouraging the youth of our community to go out into the beautiful country and enjoy recreation in the open air."

Shoemaker proposed turning the Linnaean Hill house into a museum, to "care for all things of interest pertaining to the park, its acquisition, and history . . . ." As for his family's mill, it could serve as a shelter for park visitors during thunderstorms, "or for dancing purposes."[16] As Shoemaker noted, streetcar tracks were being laid north on both sides of the park, and it was only a few minutes' walk from the stations.

In fact, as it was reported at about the same time, District authorities already had a plan "to put the old mill into commission again," though instead of grinding grain, the authorities wanted to get the wheel running as a picturesque feature in the park (the extra water brought up by the wheel would be used to sprinkle the nearby dirt roads and keep dust down during dry spells). Between 1903 and 1904, the Rock Creek board ordered

The Association of Oldest Inhabitants of the District of Columbia celebrate the Fourth of July at Louis Shoemaker's estate on Georgia Avenue, ca. 1911. Shoemaker is standing at center with his hat in hand. *Courtesy Historical Society of Washington, D.C.*

The crib-style dam used to provide water for the Peirce Mill waterwheel in the mill's final years as a commercial operation, 1899. *Courtesy Library of Congress Prints and Photographs Division.*

construction of a large concrete and boulder dam only yards from the mill, to replace the historic mill dam upstream that had been washed out. This new dam, with a seven-foot waterfall, was erected as an "attractive feature of the park," the board later reported, not as a means of trapping water for a potential new mill wheel. In any event, the larger plan for the mill's restoration depended on more congressional funding, the *Star* noted.[17]

Congressional funding remained meager, and expansive plans to restore parts of the mill were put aside, as the board's engineers did what they were trained to do: blast, dig, build, and remove. While Shoemaker was all in favor of roads, bridges, paths, and other conveniences—it benefited his real estate business and his Brightwood constituents—he was upset by the brutish manner in which the board's contractors removed the remnants of the Rock Creek milling industry, including the ruined walls of the Blagden and White mills (both located upstream from Peirce Mill), not to mention the Peirce sawmill's foundations and race. In an address to the Columbia Historical Society in 1908, Shoemaker warned that if "this devastation of relics continues, the last evidence of the once thrifty commerce, business, and utilization of water power along the line of this stream will have disappeared forever."

The screened porch of the Peirce Mill "teahouse," shortly before it was torn down as part of the restoration of the mill in 1935. *Courtesy Library of Congress Prints and Photographs Division.*

In the address, Shoemaker repeated his suggestion that Linnaean Hill be converted into a visitors center and museum. He seems to have forgiven the government officials with whom he argued over his family's property: Why not place in the reception hall of the center, he asked, "pictures of the gentlemen who at the great sacrifice to their personal interest served the government for more than a year in the acquisition of the land?" In any event, "by this time, the principle purpose declared in the act of Congress (creating Rock Creek Park) should be realized, i.e., that the land shall be a pleasure ground for the benefit of the people."[18]

Although the park's development was slow by Shoemaker's measure, the mill was a busy crossroads. One Sunday in April 1910, an astounding ten thousand people passed by—on foot and horseback, in horse-drawn carriages, on bicycles and motorcycles, and in cars. Several years earlier, an enterprising businesswoman had persuaded the board to let her sell refreshments at the mill during the warmer months. Restrooms were built across the road. Later, as more formal dining was offered, the mill became known as a "teahouse." Regular dances were held on the mill's old wooden floors, and it was so popular that couples gathered as late as December in the unheated stone building.

Bicyclists at the bridge over Rock Creek at Peirce Mill, ca. 1900. In the distance are the miller's house, *right,* and former distillery. *Courtesy Library of Congress Prints and Photographs Division.*

A later government study of the "teahouse period" concluded that "administration of the mill seems to have been quite casual." From 1909 to 1918, the Rock Creek board granted the refreshment concession at no charge to the women who operated the facility. "What changes were made in the mill during this unbusiness-like administration is a matter of conjecture," the study's author wrote. This lack of record-keeping would plague later restoration efforts seeking to maintain historical authenticity.[19]

Louis P. Shoemaker died suddenly on November 24, 1916, at sixty years of age. The *Star* praised his "progressive spirit" and leadership in the city's growth.[20] He was buried in Rock Creek Cemetery (located more than two miles from the park), where Joshua Peirce and his wife, and their son, Joshua Klingle, were also buried. The old family graveyard, on the hill above the mill, had been abandoned as a place of burial decades earlier. With Shoemaker's death, the family's 120 years of direct involvement with the mill concluded.

The clan's interest in the mill did not fade, though, in part because a Peirce cousin was living with his family at Cloverdale, a few hundred feet from the park's boundary. In keeping with the practice throughout Washington and adjoining states, park facilities were officially segregated. In 1920, an African-American woman, Hattie Sewell, got the teahouse concession. Cloverdale's inhabitants weren't happy. The Peirce cousin, Enos Newman, wrote to the control board that the teahouse was "becoming a rendezvous for colored people, developing into a nuisance."* Sewell's contract was not renewed, and the concession was turned over to the Girl Scouts.[21]

Class prejudice, too, figured as authorities on the government's oversight board during this period debated what to do with the mill. In 1918, supervision of the park had been transferred to the U.S. War Department's Office of Public Buildings and Grounds, and it soon launched a study of possible restoration strategies. The architect asked to report on the subject suggested that a mill wheel could be installed where the old wheel had been located, and run by waterpower, to give the place the appearance of antiquity. But the overriding assumption was that Peirce Mill would remain a place for casual dining and socializing for the foreseeable future.

However, it would not be *too* casual: "The introduction of a soda fountain with the usual miscellaneous assortment of candies, crackerjack and such things would, it is believed, attract a crowd which would not only afford no support to the real purpose of the place, but

---

* Newman did not specify the nature of the "nuisance." When the white woman who ran it (before Ms. Sewell) was evicted for poor service, 250 empty whiskey bottles were found on the premises.[22]

A couple enjoys a picnic at the Peirce Mill dam, ca. 1920.
Courtesy Library of Congress Prints and Photographs Division.

would serve as a detriment to the development, transforming it from a restoration with a distinct atmosphere, to an 'old mill' of the Coney Island type," the architect wrote.[23]

Also rejected during that period was a proposal by a local entrepreneur to make Peirce Mill a functioning mill once again. "It seems to me that from a business standpoint it would be a most unprofitable undertaking for you," wrote Colonel Clarence O. Sherrill, the Army officer in charge of the park, to the aspiring mill operator.[24]

The mill still had the power to inspire people intrigued with the preindustrial life. But it would take an initiative from the federal government to get the millstones grinding again at Rock Creek.

9

A New Deal for Peirce Mill

WHEN FRANKLIN D. ROOSEVELT took the presidential oath of office in March 1933, Peirce Mill had not operated for more than thirty-five years, beyond the recollections of many who lived in Washington. It was better known as the "teahouse," and the addition of a screened porch for patrons, combined with the loss of the waterwheel, obscured the building's original purpose. The new, decorative dam built directly across Rock Creek at the mill served only to create a pleasant-looking waterfall, confusing anyone trying to figure out how the mill had operated. The mill's original dam, which directed creek flow through the headrace to the waterwheel, was in ruins several hundred feet upstream.

Rock Creek's other mills were gone. Most had been scavenged for stone, and the remains had been removed to restore the park's natural landscape. For many Americans, the extraordinary inventions and conveniences developed since the 1890s—electricity, the automobile, the telephone—seemed to erase all but academic interest in such antique notions as water-powered machinery. Though a few grist mills still operated in the countryside of Virginia and Maryland, the prevailing attitude about these relics seemed to be: if it is old and in the way, why keep it?

"I think it is a mistake to assume that the building known as Pierce Mill should be perpetually kept in all respects as it was found when the park was purchased," wrote an engineer with the Rock Creek board in 1914, after receiving criticism for filling in the mill's headrace.[1]

There were advocates for keeping at least the memory of the mills alive. In November 1927, the Columbia Historical Society of Washington, D.C., heard Allen C. Clark, a noted authority on the federal city, read a paper on "the old mills" of Washington and its close-in suburbs. Clark identified more than two dozen inactive mills, many in ruins, and mentioned Peirce Mill in his straightforward account of what was known about the landmarks. Clark's address was more an exercise in nostalgia than advocacy for preservation. He included several sentimental poems about the milling world, which despite their appeal to generations past, underlined its fading presence:

Ere dawn his ghostly figure thrids
Deep avenues of sacks:
Responsive to his measured stride
The seasoned flooring cracks.

—from "The Miller" by John Cook[2]

Yet the very existence of the Columbia Historical Society (which was founded in 1894), and its desire to maintain memories, was, in fact, evidence of a national spirit opposed to the throwaway mentality beginning to dominate America. The country's formal historic preservation movement was born just before the Civil War, only a few miles south of Peirce Mill, when the Mount Vernon Ladies Association organized to save the deteriorating mansion of the revered George Washington. Later, in Boston, the Society for the Preservation of New England Antiquities was formed through the effort to maintain Paul Revere's house. The New England group also campaigned to save the houses of the less famous when the dwellings served as exemplars of a certain architectural style.* In the late 1920s, Colonial Williamsburg, the audacious effort to recreate Virginia's first capital, was funded by the private philanthropy of John D. Rockefeller. Meanwhile, the federal government became involved in conservation with congressional passage of the Antiquities Act in 1906, spurred by concern over the destruction of prehistoric sites in the Southwest. In 1916, Congress approved legislation setting up the National Park Service.[3]

The arrival of Roosevelt and his New Dealers in Washington empowered the National Park Service to reach beyond conservation of natural spaces to restoration of historic structures. A reorganization that brought Rock Creek Park under Park Service control focused more attention on Peirce Mill. In March 1934, Park Service officials proposed to Roosevelt's dynamic secretary of the interior, Harold L. Ickes, that both the mill and the Linnaean Hill house be restored.

Nicknamed the "righteous pilgrim," Ickes was a Republican progressive leader who made his reputation as an energetic reformer in the tough, gritty world of Chicago politics. His

---

*It was this same devotion to the aesthetic value of old buildings (in addition to pride in his own family) that fueled Louis Shoemaker's passion to maintain the mill and Linnaean Hill. His public appeals also came as genealogical record hunting took hold among the upper class, and the Daughters of the American Revolution and kindred groups formed to celebrate the nation's earlier history. As historians have noted, there was more than a little political and social significance to this phenomenon, coming as it did at a time when immigration and the freedom of formerly enslaved Americans provoked alarm among the Anglo-Saxon majority.

Architect Thomas Waterman, who directed the restoration of the Peirce Mill building in the 1930s, undated photograph. *Courtesy Library of Congress Prints and Photographs Division.*

conservationist perspective included visions of a Park Service domain incorporating vast new lands, particularly in the West. Ickes was also administrator of Roosevelt's public works program, formed to address massive unemployment during the Great Depression. He had the manpower and budget to tackle the Peirce Mill restoration, and the idea fit his view of what the parks were all about.

"The greatest service that we can do people who come to our parks is to get them back to the simpler things of life," Ickes told his staff in November 1934. Referring to the Roaring Twenties and the Jazz Age, only a few years earlier, he said parks could help people "eliminate all of the hectic over living that all of us have indulged in to too great an extent."[4]

For planning the restoration of the mill building and features on the grounds of the complex (as distinct from the milling machinery), the Park Service used a promising young architect, Thomas T. Waterman. Raised in New York City, Waterman was drawn to building design as a teenager. He skipped college and went directly from prep school to the prestigious Boston architectural firm of Cram, Goodhue & Ferguson, where he was trained as a draftsman. Soon, Waterman met and came under the influence of William Sumner Appleton, founder of the Society for the Preservation of New England Antiquities. Waterman was one of the first draftsmen hired for the Colonial Williamsburg project, and he helped design the Wren Building and other restored structures at the former Virginia capital. By the time Harold Ickes endorsed a restoration of Peirce Mill, Waterman was busy with numerous projects in the mid-Atlantic states.

"Waterman recommended honoring the various stages of a building's life, as opposed to the literal replication of its earliest known form," a study of his work noted. Even trim from various periods on a building, if authentic, "should be allowed to remain as part of the history of a structure," Waterman believed. Restorers should "do as little disruptive work as possible, to retain any existing old work, to repair rather than replace, and to save all unused parts." If new work was necessary, Waterman argued for "blending rather than 'faking,' and distinguishing new work from the original."[5]

This outlook suited Peirce Mill, whose interior had been altered through the decades as technology and millers changed, and water and other elements rotted wooden machinery. Records were scant, making it hard to identify exactly when certain components and systems had been replaced, and who had done the work.

In their effort to track down information on the mill, Park Service officials located Francis Shoemaker, Pierce Shoemaker's only surviving son, who was living in a Washington hotel. They took him to the mill in November 1934 to see what he might recall. Unlike his brother Louis, Francis had opted for the blue-collar life, apparently working at the mill until it stopped operating in 1897. Then, using his family inheritance, he became a collector of cigar store life-size wooden Indians.

Francis Shoemaker's initial comments concerned the miller's office. Walking in the door on the western-facing side of the building, he indicated the formerly partitioned area, and the desk where the books were kept and where business was transacted "in the old days," according to an account by Ruth Butler, a Park Service historian who was there that day. On the desk, which was still in its place, were the initials and dates of employment of Alcibiades White, the last man to operate the mill.

Two millstones remained in their hoops (metal holding rings) on a raised section of the same floor. The oldest was made of flint and intended for grinding corn. The other stone, a French "buhr" for grinding wheat, was bought in 1880 by Shoemaker. These expensive stones, which American millers prized for their hardness, came from a granite quarry near Paris. Although the mill had three sets of stones, "Mr. Shoemaker declared that the water power had never been sufficient for turning more than two at a time," according to Butler's account.

Butler herself could not resist marveling at a "simple yet ingenious piece of machinery for removing grains of corn from their cobs" found on the second floor. It was a cylinder of wood "from which projects large wooden teeth, irregularly spaced. As this cylinder revolves, the grains are detached and fall into a container while the smooth cob falls out of a small aperture on the lower-left side."[6]

Butler also had interviewed Shoemaker before the visit to the mill. Unfortunately, the record of that conversation could not be found. In all, it appears that while Shoemaker added a few important details to the information base used by the restoration team, the project would still involve a good deal of guesswork.

Thomas Waterman began planning for work on the mill building a few months before the Shoemaker interview, making drawings and photographs, and conducting his own research into the mill's history. In a press release of January 1935, the Park Service announced the project, stating "that unless Pierce Mill is restored now, its identity will be lost and its preservation seriously jeopardized." The announcement added that "extreme care has been taken to make it a true copy of the original mill."[7]

To the contrary, Waterman did not believe in making "true copies," and few records existed to document the mill's original state. Nevertheless, every effort was made to obtain and use authentic parts. First, Waterman had the easy work done, pointing stonework on the exterior, which included repair of the chimney. Cement window stools were replaced with stone, and the teahouse addition removed. Later, a new roof was put on using hand-split cedar shingles. Nineteenth-century hardware was found for the doors, and a stove thought to date from about 1820 was obtained for the miller's office. Work on the building was almost finished by the summer of 1935.

For fabrication of the milling machinery, the Park Service contracted with the Fitz Water Wheel Company of Hanover, Pennsylvania. Founded in 1840, Fitz was one of a handful of manufacturers in the United States that still made authentic wooden mill wheels. Owner John S. Fitz, a wire-thin man who was the third generation in his family to run the firm, believed there was no reason why Americans could not continue using waterpower, especially if they lived in the East, with its abundant rivers and creeks. But it helped if a customer had an aversion to electricity, as did Fitz's Amish neighbors, who kept him in business. "If you want to see what small batches of raindrops are doing for hundreds of farmers, and could do for thousands, with little cost or care, visit the Pennsylvania Germans," Fitz told a reporter.[8]

For Peirce Mill, Fitz ordered his staff to scavenge parts from mills around the region to use in the repairs and construction. Gears turned up in Pennsylvania and Maryland. The valuable, early-nineteenth-century "hopper boy" (a mechanical device that cooled hot, freshly ground flour), came from a mill in Baltimore County. "It's probably the last machine of its type in existence today," Fitz said.

Other old parts were still at hand in Washington: the big millstones, the gigantic wooden frame that supported the milling machinery, wooden elevators, mechanisms that cleaned grain and sifted flour. Fitz's staff fabricated a new "breast wheel," the type of wooden wheel that probably was used at Peirce Mill prior to installation of the turbine. A breast wheel is powered by both the weight of the water in the buckets and the force of the water striking the buckets.

Fitz would have preferred a more efficient steel overshot wheel, but such an arrangement would have been more difficult to run, given the relatively low flow of Rock Creek. A new mill race bringing water from upstream to the wheel was dug near the old trench, which had been filled in twenty years earlier. About six feet across and more than three hundred feet long, the race was neatly lined with cut stone, a more attractive look than that of the historical, rugged, rock-filled channel. The owners of a commercial milling operation normally would not spend the money necessary to make the headrace a work of art.

The Peirce Mill headrace built during the New Deal restoration. The headrace carried water from upstream to the waterwheel, which cannot be seen in this 1950 photograph. *Courtesy Library of Congress Prints and Photographs Division.*

Waterman wanted to build a new timber crib dam upstream. This style of dam, a wood-framed structure filled with rocks, would be based on one that had been documented at Peirce Mill at the end of the nineteenth century. Its chief virtue was a more dependable and sufficient head of water. No funds had been designated for this part of the project, so Waterman had to accept a "boulder" dam, which was a long pile of rocks fashioned from existing rubble already in the creek. The boulder dam "is not in harmony with the stone work of Pierce Mill or with traditional mill dams," Waterman wrote to a colleague.[9] The first boulder structure was too low to produce a sufficient flow of water to power all three millstones at once. Evidently, money was eventually found to raise the level of the rock dam.

As construction of the milling machinery neared completion in the spring of 1936, Fitz was still searching for an all-important set of authentic mill scales—"weight" historically being the locus of so much haggling as well as the determinant of a miller's reputation. Fitz located one set of scales at a mill in Hershey, Pennsylvania; ironically, although he had a persuasive, confident personality, he could not convince the owner to part with the device.

Another 1950 view of the Peirce Mill headrace looking north to where it took in water from Rock Creek. *Courtesy Library of Congress Prints and Photographs Division.*

Fitz's self-assurance was demonstrated in a letter to the Park Service written as the project got underway. Fitz maintained that the "designs we have submitted will conform more closely with the best milling practices in existence a century ago." Several other notes confirm his confidence that what he planned would be in keeping with the "old mill," and that his methods were "undoubtedly used by Isaac Pierce." To further assure park managers, Fitz emphasized that one of his consultants was an eighty-four-year-old Maryland engineer who at age fourteen, just after the Civil War, had been apprenticed to a well-regarded Virginia millwright.[10] Such a pedigree, Fitz seemed to be suggesting, was the closest thing to actually using Peirce for the job.

Testing and tinkering went on at the mill for several more months. On a cold, rainy afternoon in January 1937, forty years after the turbine shaft shattered and ended the mill's commercial life, Peirce Mill opened as an historic educational project of the National Park Service. Despite the discouraging weather, more than 2,400 people showed up to watch Robert Little,

an itinerant miller hired by the park, operate the restored wooden machinery and millstones. At precisely 1:00 p.m., the headrace gate was opened, sending a gush of water to the new mill wheel. To celebrate the event, government employees gave away more than one thousand pounds of flour ground by Little, dressed in a white cap and long white jacket. The next day, a story on the front page of the *Washington Post* chronicled the opening.

Little, who was about sixty years old, had worked in mills across the country since his youth and "liked the idea of getting the old place moving," according to the *Post* account. "He said the rumble of rollers and the whisk of belt over pulley was music to his ears."

The two-year restoration, completed for $26,624, was one of the Park Service's first major efforts at historic preservation. And it proved popular: in its first year of operation, the mill sold more than three thousand pounds of cornmeal and seven hundred pounds of wheat flour in one-pound and five-pound bags. The freshly ground product also was marketed to government cafeterias around the capital. "Flour will be sold to keep the mill on a self-supporting basis," the *Post* reported.[11]

Some Interior Department employees were enchanted with having their own mill in Washington. One was moved to write poetry:

> A wonder of the simple time of old
> When machines were of the rarest mark.
> So we of these enlightened times
> See once again as our forefathers saw
> And hear old Pierce's mill at work again.[12]

A few in the city's press corps, however, found the entire enterprise laughable. They started poking fun at the revived mill even before it was completed. "The antiquated machinery, bolstered by new materials, will begin to wheeze in the same . . . manner of James Monroe's day," a reporter wrote in the conservative *Washington Times-Herald*. It was "New Deal boondoggling" to repair the "village queen," the newspaper declared in February 1936.[13]

A wire-service writer turned the story into a satire that cast Interior Secretary Ickes as a worried miller, hoping the ice would thaw in his mill pond so he could get the wheel turning again. The story mixed up the facts and concocted a few of its own, concluding: "It will be the most expensive flour, perhaps, ever ground in history and Ickes doesn't know where to peddle it."[14]

The Park Service did devise a plan to sell the flour, but exactly how the Peirce Mill project became a small commercial operation remains a mystery. An article in mid-1935 quoted one government official as saying "that everyone was a little vague as to the purpose of the

Rebuilding the Peirce Mill sluice and waterwheel, 1935.
Courtesy National Park Service.

Workers at Peirce Mill's decorative dam, 1937. *Courtesy National Park Service.*

restoration, except to restore it." Fitz stated the same year that his milling machinery was "capable of grinding wheat flour [and] cornmeal," though he was aiming to make Peirce Mill "an exhibit of ancient mill machinery."[15]

Before the mill reopened, a consultant hired by the Park Service indicated that the mill could be run at a slight profit if it sold cornmeal and whole wheat flour to retail customers visiting the park. Production of white flour was not part of the plan, since millstones were unable to produce a grade comparable to that manufactured by modern roller mills. The consultant, advocating for natural foods decades before it became fashionable to do so, noted that "nutritionists and dieticians are well aware of the superiority of this coarsely ground meal" over white flour.[16]

Interior Secretary Ickes, meanwhile, was having second thoughts about his mill project. In early 1936, Ickes summoned the acting director of the Park Service, Arthur E. Demaray, to his office and read a newspaper article criticizing the mill restoration as an extravagance. Ickes, of course, was sensitive to the politics of such coverage; Roosevelt was beginning his first re-election campaign. Demaray later recalled Ickes' suggestion "that there ought to be a ready market for water-ground meal which could be sold in fancy packages to the public at a price which would pay for the operation of the mill." Demaray said he replied that it would useful to bring in the War Department recreational association since it could run the mill during the day and schoolchildren could see it in operation. "You [Ickes] authorized me to see what I could arrange," Demaray recalled.[17]

In January 1937, after Roosevelt's landslide re-election, and as the mill reopened, Ickes again raised concerns about its expanded mission, writing Demaray: "I recall distinctly that it was I who first suggested the restoration of the mill, but I never expected it to be operated and I did not know that it was going to be operated." Now Ickes seemed to be fretting about the frustrations of running a large bureaucracy: "Here was a policy evolved over a course of months without the matter being brought to my attention even by way of a memorandum of information."

Ickes curtly rejected Demaray's invitation to preside over a second opening ceremony at the mill, with Washington schoolchildren in attendance: "The mill has in fact been dedicated by being thrown open to the public. Another dedication does not seem to me to be called for."[18] As much as the milling operation upset him, Ickes did not move to halt the grinding of grain for commercial sale, and so was born Peirce Mill's unusual role as an historical site intended to pay for itself.

Robert Little, hired chiefly to operate the mill, provided some basic information to visitors, but in those early years the Park Service provided only rudimentary historical interpretation at the site. Congress had authorized the Park Service to open museums and erect historic markers. The aim was to breathe life into American history "for those to whom is has been a dull recital of meaningless facts—to recreate for the average citizen something of the color, the pageantry, and the dignity of our national past," wrote Verne Chatelain, the Park Service's first chief historian. "There is no more effective way of teaching history to the average American than to take him to the site on which some great historic event has occurred."

No great events occurred at Peirce Mill; all along, the rationale for the restoration was to demonstrate a venerable technology key to the American story. It was a straightforward tale, showing that "our history is a series of processes marked by certain stages of development . . . certain levels of growth," Chatelain argued.[19] The time had not yet come to critique growth, to show how it was achieved through the callous exploitation of people or nature. Part of the Peirce Mill story could be seen in that light, but such interpretation was decades away.

Robert Little, the first miller at the restored Peirce Mill, ca. 1937. *Courtesy National Park Service.*

10

Space Age Mill?

IN PEIRCE MILL'S EARLY YEARS UNDER PARK SERVICE MANAGEMENT, the grounds nearby served as a setting for campfire programs, nature walks, and other standard outdoors fare. Large numbers of visitors used the field across the street for picnics and baseball. The mill continued to supply government cafeterias with flour, and—if you believe one miller's recollections—the White House, as well.

Within a short time, however, it became apparent that the raised boulder dam was directing creek water such that it inundated the low ground adjoining the mill, depositing silt and destroying vegetation. In 1940, a completely new dam to supply water for the headrace was proposed, at an estimated cost of $25,000. Those funds could not be found, so the dam may have been lowered by simply removing some of the rocks, imperiling the water supply necessary to turn all the millstones at once.

During World War II, the mill began to lose money due to wartime price controls and restrictions on sales to the public. The restrictions came after the owners of the Chapman Mill near Gainesville, Virginia, more than forty miles away, complained to Senator Harry F. Byrd Jr. that their business was suffering from the competition from Peirce Mill flour.[1] It was a dubious allegation, but such was the power of the Virginia Democrat that the Roosevelt administration had to pay attention to the request for relief.

The miller during the war, a former carpet layer named B. H. Didawick, threatened to quit in early 1943 unless he got a pay raise. "I'm a kickin' and I'm quittin' if they don't raise my salary. I'll retire to my farm in the valley of Virginia," the sixty-six-year-old Didawick told the *Evening Star*.[2]

For the two decades after the 1936 opening, the millwheel and millstones only operated during colder months, for lack of refrigeration to preserve the flour. At peak output, the mill produced about two tons of flour annually. The mill's intermittent disuse caused the wheel

Miller Raymond Watt filling bags containing Peirce Mill product, ca. 1940s. Watt worked at the mill from 1940 to 1966. *Courtesy National Park Service. Below,* Peirce Mill bag.

to dry and then warp and crack. By 1958, "machinery breakdown, fluctuations in the water supply, and the unavailability of trained millwrights" led to an indefinite shutdown of the waterwheel, a history of Rock Creek Park noted.[3]

Even after being deprived of a mill to run, that era's folksy miller, Raymond Watt, continued to work as a guide. Watt, a former auto mechanic, had acquired some experience at a steam-driven mill. In the tradition of Robert Little, Watt was not required to work in a period costume appropriate to the mill's early-nineteenth-century era, nor did he have to train as an historical interpreter. Peirce Mill did acquire its first full-time park ranger in the late 1950s, when John Wolf was transferred to the site from his post at the Lincoln Memorial. Wolf "did a lot of historical research on the mill, and formulated the first interpretive programs," recalled a former Park Service staff member.[4]

Nevertheless, this was the dawn of the Space Age, as well as a period when prepared baking mixes were widely popular. Would the attraction of modern technology and ready-to-eat products once again cause authorities to leave the mill behind? Ray Watt was not optimistic. "All the women work, and when they come home they warm something to put on the table. Nobody has the time to bake anymore. Another twenty years, women won't know how to cook," he told a reporter.[5]

"PIERCE MILL MAKES Fine Health Flour" was the headline of a story in the *Washington Times-Herald* of February 1940. The newspaper's recipe editor reported that managers of the mill had produced "special bread that contains the live wheat germ, one of the few natural sources of the precious Vitamin E." She added: "I'm terribly proud that we're making this health-giving bread right here in Washington from whole wheat ground in one of the most historic mills in the country. It gives me sort of a patriotic thrill when I think about it." The proprietary recipe for the health loaf was not supplied, but the article included:

Quick Buckwheat Cakes

1 ½ cups buckwheat

½ cup white flour

1 teaspoon salt

3 teaspoons baking powder

1 ¾ cups milk

1 egg

Sift buckwheat, flour, salt, and baking powder. Add egg, well-beaten, then gradually add milk. Beat well to remove all lumps and cook at once on a hot greased griddle. Two tablespoons of black molasses may be added before cooking, if desired. This helps to brown cakes and sweeten them as well.[6]

Miller Raymond Watt at the first floor hopper, ca. 1940s. *Courtesy National Park Service.*

While old-time cooking skills may have been falling out of favor, the preservation movement was growing, spurred by the birth of the National Trust for Historic Preservation in 1949. And nationwide, mills had articulate and widely published advocates. New England artist and antique tool collector Eric Sloane, in a mid-1950's article for the prestigious magazine *American Heritage*, argued that the miller's "place in the fabric of our history is distinct":

The miller was America's first industrial inventor. He was builder, banker, businessman and host to the countryside. When highways were no wider than today's bridle paths, the first good roads were built to the mills. Where there was a mill site, there was a nucleus for a town. America had so many Millvilles, Milltowns, Milfords, and other towns named after original mills, that the Post Office Department sponsored the changing of many such names to stop the confusion.[7]

A few years later, rising interest in the historic milling experience would spawn the Society for the Preservation of Old Mills, a national nonprofit organization whose members included mill owners, museum curators, antique machinery buffs, and other devotees of the fast-disappearing profession (despite the dominance of Midwest grain and flour conglomerates, a few individual mills had held on and still made flour the old-fashioned way).[8]

The 1960s saw the preservation movement widen to include entire neighborhoods or districts. "If we wish to have a future with greater meaning," a 1965 report by the U.S. Conference of Mayors declared, "we must concern ourselves not only with the historic highlights," but with the "total heritage of the nation." This could be a village green, or an early industrial site such as a mill village. Preservation legislation passed by Congress in 1966 created a "National Register of Historic Places" authorized to designate sites worth keeping, and within three years, Peirce Mill was nominated for the register.[9]

The mill and other Peirce buildings at the intersection of Rock Creek and Tilden Street, though never recognized together as a separate historic district, did constitute an area of unusual authenticity that the Park Service would strive to preserve. The springhouse, the oldest documented structure, remained intact on a stretch of greensward separating Tilden's east and west routes. Across the street was Cloverdale, altered but still reminiscent of the world of Pierce Shoemaker. The home would be owned by his descendants until the 1980s. Nearer the mill were the Peirces' stone carriage house and the building known as the distillery. The latter had been enlarged to serve as a private home, but retained its distinctive character.

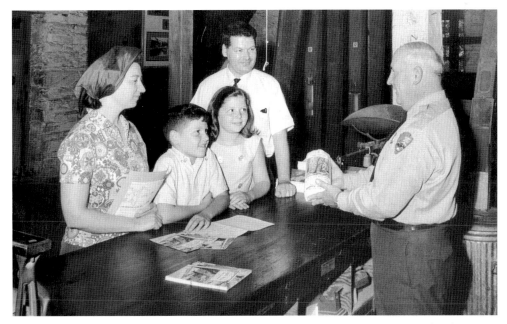

Park Ranger John Wolf explains Peirce Mill operation to visitors, 1965. *Courtesy National Park Service.*

Even with heightened interest in historic preservation, it took more than a decade after the mill wheel broke in 1958 to get it turning again. Peirce Mill ranger John Wolf was described in one newspaper article in the mid-1960s as "the most lonesome guide in the local National Park Service system . . . yawning there at his solitary post with his manually operated, push-button people counter." On some weekdays, fewer than a half-dozen visitors came to the idle mill. To keep busy, Wolf did some of the early work on a restoration plan before leaving for a new job in West Virginia. Early in 1965, John Fitz, more than eighty years old and still on the job at his Pennsylvania company, drove down to Washington to inspect the machinery he had installed three decades earlier. He estimated that it would cost nearly $10,000 to build and install a new wheel. The old wheel "probably would still be in usable condition today if it had been kept in operation, and if the tail race had not been allowed to fill up with mud and submerge the lower part of the waterwheel," Fitz informed the Park Service.

Before the Park Service could decide how to proceed, Fitz died and his firm shut down. Perhaps sensing weakness on the part of the building's stewards, rock-throwing vandals repeatedly broke the mill's windows.[10]

In the end, the Park Service decided to handle the mill repairs in-house. Again, changes were made in the water system and wheel style. The millrace had proven a maintenance burden; flooding would clog it with sediment and debris. Nor was it able to deliver water at a consistent volume. So, that quasi-historical feature was buried, but not before a pipe was laid along its length to draw water from the creek, upstream. This flow was enhanced by a pump attached to a new source—city tap water. An overshot wheel, considered by some park officials to be historically accurate since that configuration could have been used in the mid-nineteenth century, was installed, with the outflow dumped through the tailrace into Rock Creek.[11]

Environmentally, this was ill-advised; chlorinated water kills fish. Financially, it could have been a budget-breaker, though apparently the Park Service was not charged for the water. From an interpretive standpoint, filling in the millrace undermined the entire site's historical accuracy, since it misrepresented how water-powered mills operated in their heyday.[12]

In the midst of the restoration, a local millwright was consulted. Scrutinizing the work underway, he declared that, "due to the wrong technical procedure and extremely unauthentic advice given you, I strongly recommend abandoning any further expenditure on the present program" at Peirce Mill. To get the mill operating without what the consultant termed "phony" designs and features would cost the Park Service $75,000.[13]

Park managers decided not to spend that money (a decision that may have been linked to perennial budgetary shortfalls throughout the Park Service), and by the summer of 1970, the mill wheel was operating under city waterpower. Two years later, Hurricane Agnes, the worst storm ever to hit the East Coast, swamped the area; in a twenty-four-hour period, more than

Peirce Mill's overshot millwheel in the 1960s. *Courtesy National Park Service.*

Boy Scouts help with a clean-up at Peirce Mill, August 1965. *Courtesy National Park Service.*

Young visitors try out a model mill at Peirce Mill in the 1970s. *Courtesy National Park Service.*

ten inches of rain inundated the Washington region. Rock Creek rose high enough to lap the mill's back door, sending water into the basement. The flood coated the walls and floor with bacteria-laden residue from the polluted creek. It took weeks of cleaning and repairs before the mill could reopen.

In 1973, an estimated 93,500 people came to watch the gears turn inside the mill, the highest annual turnout in a decade that saw more than a half million visitors tour the site. The mill's popularity stemmed in part from "living history" programs featuring volunteers in period costume demonstrating skills and customs from the era before electricity. On a Sunday in January 1973, about five hundred people visited the mill, some tasting corn fritters cooked on a wooden stove by a government secretary dressed in handmade gingham. Nearby, another volunteer used a hand-turned corn shucker. Visitors enjoyed the scene as pure nostalgia, or a bargain hunter's delight. "It's a very good buy, thirty cents a pound [for cornmeal]," said one woman.

During the 1970s, Robert Batte, a retired Washington, D.C., bus driver, was hired to run the machinery. Although he was the son of a West Virginia miller and had gained some experience working for his father, Batte had more in common with his predecessor, Raymond Watt. Both were hired because they were mechanically minded. Historic interpretation was not part of the job description—that role was for the park ranger on duty. Batte also echoed

Watt's complaints about household roles, telling a reporter, "I take cornmeal and flour home myself. Make whole wheat biscuits and corn bread. Bake it myself. My wife's too modern."[14]

Popular as the mill was in the 1970s, the in-house, patch-up job of the previous decade was already causing problems. In 1977, the Park Service asked English millwright Derek Ogden to examine Peirce Mill and recommend ways to improve its operation. A native of Stratford-on-Avon, Ogden was taught how to repair mills by his grandfather, and became an internationally known authority, working on mill projects in France, Tasmania, South Africa, and India. Drawn to the United States by a demand for mill experts, Ogden recently had begun work at the Flowerdew Hundred plantation on Virginia's James River.

During his initial years in America, Ogden directed the construction of a replica at Flowerdew of the first English-style windmill built in Virginia. His quest for accuracy included arranging for sixty tons of English oak to be shipped to the site. For restoration projects, he was adamant about working with the remaining structures fabricated by earlier millwrights, rather than imposing a modern sensibility.

"You must try to make the repairs in the same spirit in which the mill was made," he told one interviewer. "You have to believe in the romance of it, or act like a jackleg [amateur]. But if it was built by a jackleg, you have to get in a jackleg mode and do it that way." Ogden added: "You can always tell a good millwright by the way he hid his mistakes. When I work on a mill I feel I know the man who built it two or three hundred years ago. He is very real. I know exactly what the man was like though we have never met."[15]

Ogden, who did his work by hand in his own wood shop, urged that the Peirce Mill wheel be converted back to the breast-wheel style, with the headrace restored and fed by a new dam upstream that would provide sufficient water. This would make the mill "closer to the original mechanically, hydraulically and historically than it is at present," Ogden wrote to the Park Service, adding pointedly: "The works of converting the mill to creek operation must be carefully supervised by a millwright having experience and understanding of mill works and hydraulics."[16]

The Rock Creek Park superintendent essentially endorsed Ogden's report, but the conversions never took place for lack of the estimated $82,000 it would take to make them. That decision led to more mechanical problems and in 1981, the mill wheel again stopped turning. A few years earlier, the Park Service had authorized the transformation of the Peirce family's old carriage house (next to the mill) into an art gallery. Though an admirable use of the old structure, the gallery bore no relation to the historical site, and the conversion—as with the removal of the millrace—dealt another blow to the mill site's authenticity.

Yet, more than money, what the mill needed was a champion, someone who could run the machinery, understand its particular nature and history, and at the same time communicate those things to the public.

11

A New Pennsylvanian Miller

IN 1984, AS PARK SERVICE STAFF worked on a plan to get Peirce Mill operating again, a new miller was hired. His name was Theodore Roosevelt "Ted" Hazen Jr., and he had grown up in Pennsylvania, home state of the Peirces, although he was from the northwest region near Lake Erie. Milling and water mechanics were in the family genes: Hazen's father was a laborer who had worked on mill dams, whose own father had been a plumber eventually named superintendent of the Erie municipal water works. Hazen's other grandfather was a violin maker from what is now the Slovak Republic. In the United States, that grandfather later became a millwright, even building a small mill down the street from Ted's family home.

"I guess milling got into my blood when my father used to take us to the [nearby] Drake's Mill to buy buckwheat flour. The water flowed down the mill race and operated the water turbines that ran the mill. I remember hearing the sounds of the mill operating as you walked up to the mill's loading dock," Hazen recalled during an interview in 2007.[1]

Youthful and enthusiastic, Hazen was unlike any previous miller hired by the Park Service for Peirce Mill, for he combined love for the milling life with technical expertise and historical perspective. Even before he graduated from college in the late 1970s, Hazen worked at mills in western Pennsylvania, learning the miller's trade through on-the-job training. Later, he moved to Tennessee, then South Carolina, acquiring knowledge of varied milling technologies, both wind and water, as well as new electric-powered systems. He benefited from the growing interest nationwide in the revival of old mills. While numerous relatively modern (and independent) mills were shutting down, unable to compete with the nation's major milling companies, some preindustrial mills were undergoing restoration. Public appreciation was growing for the authentic, old-style flours they produced.

The Rock Creek Park staff that Hazen joined was plagued with personnel management problems that complicated any effort to keep the mill operational. Nevertheless, Hazen credited Georgia Ellard, Rock Creek Park's superintendent in the 1980s, with getting the mill reopened and running once again. Ellard "considered the mill just as important as the Old Stone House, the Carter Barron Amphitheatre, the Nature Center," and other features of the park, Hazen said. Jack Fish, another senior official in the Park Service's regional staff, also "loved the mill," and helped put Hazen to work there.

When he started work at Peirce Mill, Hazen says, he restored the flour bolter and built a grain elevator, bin, chute, and conveyor. The sack hoist, which hauls grain to the third floor, operated for the first time in recent memory, and Hazen reinstalled the smutter, a mechanism that cleans grain before it is ground. Hazen believed he got most of the automated system invented by Oliver Evans working again, including the so-called "hopper boy" mechanism used to cool flour fresh from the millstones. In the process, he realized that the city water system barely delivered enough propulsive power to run the equipment. The underpowered arrangement and the single set of millstones meant that he could not grind grain and send the result up the elevator fast enough. Instead, flour slid back down the shaft, jamming the system. He had to run the mill in stages, noncontinuously.

Tall and husky, sporting a beard and wire-rimmed glasses, Hazen also knew instinctively how to entertain visitors. "I'm a clown," he admitted. "Put me in front of an audience and I'll draw a crowd." As a noncareer Park Service employee, he gave rules and regulations short shrift at times. His take on the mill's history sometimes veered from known facts. But a good miller was hard to find, so park officials, cognizant of Hazen's talents, tolerated his unconventional behavior.

The mill had three pairs of millstones on site, including a set of four-foot-wide French buhrs that Hazen returned to service. However, it took an outside consultant to diagnose the millstones' chief problem: when installed in the 1970s, their furrows—the grinding edges—were set to run backward. The buhr stones, which American millers valued for their hardness, had not been used in thirty years at Peirce Mill. "They were a great pair of millstones that had been purchased from a dealer in Georgetown" in the nineteenth century, Hazen said. "The stone of that diameter, and weight, ground grain wonderfully."

The mill also had a pair of Pennsylvania conglomerate millstones, installed in the 1970s. Of smaller diameter, these stones could grind nearly as well as the French millstones, according to Hazen. "I used it to grind most days since it was easier to lift by myself using the millstone crane, and clean up after grinding demonstrations."

Among the many aspects of milling that fascinated Hazen was regional grain preferences: "In Pennsylvania, white corn was not good enough, so it was fed to the animals. In the South, white corn was for humans. In Pennsylvania, yellow corn was milled

Top, Ted Hazen, miller at Peirce Mill from 1984 to 1995, "dressing" or repairing the shearing edge of a millstone. *Courtesy National Park Service.* **Left,** Ted Hazen. *Courtesy Theodore R. Hazen Jr.* **Above,** Millwright Derek Ogden, 1997. *Courtesy Bob Leek.*

into meal, but in central and southeastern Pennsylvania, they roast it first, and then mill it, and it's known as 'Pennsylvania Dutch style.' New England folks prefer rye to wheat. For corn bread, instead of mixing in wheat or white flour they simply add rye flour to make what they call 'Rye & Injun.'"

A devoted promoter of forgotten American trades and traditions, Hazen set up a public program on early crafts that was underway by spring 1987. That season and through the summer, the site was open Wednesday through Sunday. The "Pierce Mill Spring Festival" featured stone carving, spinning, rail splitting, and basket and cabinet making. Performers offered bluegrass music and traditional American dance demonstrations. In late summer, craftspeople showed visitors how to make paper, lace, and dulcimers. In an innovative twist, Hazen installed a female spinner making thread in the Peirce springhouse situated in the middle of Tilden Street.[2]

Dressed as a Pennsylvanian laborer of the early nineteenth century—clothing he researched for historical accuracy—Hazen loved to engage children with tales of the Peirces and the history of milling. He was always ready to grind corn and wheat into grits or flour, his most popular products, and he would also put rye, oats, rice, barley, and buckwheat between the millstones.

Peirce Mill ranger Steve Strach helped Hazen by enlarging the site's historical research files—and pitching in when all the visitors had left. "Steve and I would work many nights until midnight or later cleaning the mill, or, dealing with water or flooding in the basement," Hazen said.

Some on the park management staff, however, bristled at the emphasis Hazen put on the mill's commercial role, even though it was a draw for visitors. The staff asked Hazen to

OVER THE YEARS I HAVE SEEN a wide variety of interpretation in old mills, some very good, and some very bad. I find that interpretation of old mills has two drastically different effects upon the visitor when the mill is operating versus when the mill is not operating. You could be the best interpreter in the world, but when the machinery begins to operate there is nothing like it.... Even the best interpreter has to take a second seat to the turning machinery. All one can do is add to what is already happening. It may be like witnessing creation, the raw grain going in and seeing the final flour coming out, and being able to touch it between your fingers. Who wants to read about it or hear about it when you can see the real thing happening before your eyes? It is like watching bread dough grow into a loaf of warm baked bread before your eyes. —*Types of Interpretation* by Ted Hazen[3]

Participants and a visitor at a Peirce Mill crafts festival in the 1980s. *Courtesy National Park Service.*

stop producing bran, a wheat by-product, believing it took too much time. As one ranger wrote a few years later, "One important fact to keep in mind is that Pierce Mill is a museum and historic site, not a mill. The goal [of restoration] must be preservation of an historic site, and not modernization for a more efficient mill."

The ranger endorsed the idea of a park employee wearing traditional miller's garb, and running the wheel to grind grain. But he proposed that only corn be ground, and that it be given away in small bags labeled "bird feed," a gesture he felt would eliminate worries about sanitation, ventilation, and health regulations. "The last miller employed at Pierce Mill did not regard himself as a government or NPS [National Park Service] civil servant, but rather as a miller employed by the government. This increased the problem of the site being managed as a mill rather than as an historic site."[4]

Of course, the ranger was referring to Ted Hazen. Hazen—entrepreneurial, imaginative, energetic—was an heir to the traditions of fellow Pennsylvanians Jonathan Shoemaker, Abner Cloud, and Isaac Peirce. He even had some of the inventiveness (and moodiness) of Oliver Evans, the Delaware creator of the automated mill system.

But it lay beyond Hazen's talents and duties to find the money to maintain the mill. In 1993, the waterwheel shaft broke from decay, making it unsafe to run the system.[5] At that time, approximately twenty thousand visitors, including large numbers of local elementary school children, were coming to see the mill every year. Efforts were being made to ensure that the students' visit to the mill fulfilled curriculum requirements in history and science.

The rotted wheel shaft was only the most dramatic sign of the mill's woeful condition. Posts in the basement, and the main beam above them, were weakened by rot due to frequent flooding from Rock Creek. The posts stood precariously on stone wedges. Deteriorating floor boards, windows, and machinery parts gave the structure the look not of history, but of dilapidation.

A few years after the shaft failed, the Park Service again asked Virginia-based millwright Derek Ogden to assess the situation. This time, Ogden left the politesse of his 1977 report behind: "The general appearance of the hurst frame is one of very poor twentieth century construction," he wrote, referring to the structure that holds the gears and countershafts. He noted that the wood used in the frame supporting the gears and millstones had been cut with a modern-day circular saw, rather than historically accurate hand tools. Observant visitors would recognize that shortcut.

The waterwheel system, with its tap-water supply and controls on the building's exterior, was "complete nonsense," Ogden continued. The wooden flume (a channel carrying water from the headrace to the waterwheel) was "inaccurate mechanically, historically, and traditionally because it has no associations with eighteenth or nineteenth century design or construction." Ogden also derided the maintenance—or lack—given to the milling machinery. And he was not pleased that a single set of millstones was used for wheat, corn, and buckwheat. Millers of the eighteenth and nineteenth centuries used separate, custom-grooved sets of stones for each grain and the desired flour.

Peirce Mill's saving grace was its third floor, essentially a milling museum in miniature. The "hopper boy" mechanism was "quite accurate" in its relation to Oliver Evans's specifications (though Ogden felt it was a reproduction, not a period original; as did John Fitz, who had found it back in the 1930s). A rolling screen grain cleaner also passed Ogden's inspection, as did the barrel hoist, a platform used to carry barrels of meal and flour between floors, the usual way of moving materials before the Evans elevator system became commonplace.[6]

Ogden said it would take nearly $500,000 simply to make needed machinery repairs. His blunt assessment was in keeping with the tradition of independent-minded, even abrasive, millwrights and millers (Oliver Evans had set the pace with his reputation for peevishness).* Chiefly an attack on Park Service stewardship of the mill, Ogden's analysis implicitly criticized Ted Hazen's tenure as the miller. Hazen, not surprisingly, had no use for the curmudgeonly Ogden.

---

*John Fitz's veteran millwright-consultant had written at one point, commenting on government inspectors: "Millwright work is slow at best and appears more so when compared to carpenter work . . . it looks like a millwright is trying to make his job last as long as possible, especially when a carpenters' union thinks they can do the work as good and much faster . . . this belief is born of ignorance . . . and illustrates the old adage, quote, fools will with boldness go where angels fear to tread."[7]

Other challenges had arisen at the mill site. The decorative dam, of no use to the mill's function, irritated Park Service naturalists and local environmentalists, who saw it as a major barrier to annual spawning by herring and other fish that swam up Rock Creek. The question was, could the creek's ecology, and that of the Potomac River, also elements of regional history, be restored, along with the mill?

After the shaft failed, Hazen stayed on for two more years, showing visitors as best he could how the mill would operate if it could be run. Then, the Park Service decided to eliminate the miller's job, offering him as an alternative a chance to drive trash trucks. Losing the job Hazen loved hurt, but it may have saved his life, as he had contracted a chronic infection working at the mill. "The doctor said it had gotten into my right ear from the dirt, dampness, mold, smoke and constant cleaning of the basement from contaminated creek water," Hazen recalled. "It was affecting my memory, my sense of balance, my concentration, and my eyesight." Even worse, just before the Park Service dropped the miller's position, Hazen came down with bacterial meningitis.

Hazen had grown close to a woman who worked for the Norfolk Southern railroad company in Roanoke, Virginia. Recovering from his various afflictions, he decided to move there and see if he could find work in that area's mills.

Meanwhile, the Park Service indicated Peirce Mill was near the end of the line for the limited government funds designated for Washington-area park sites. When this policy shift became clear, Richard Abbott, a volunteer who had been assisting Hazen the day the wheel shaft failed, decided to take action. He wrote a letter, prominently displayed with a photograph of the mill in winter, which appeared in the *Washington Post* in September 1996.

"This fascinating part of the history of our area should not be lost," Abbott wrote. "I would be willing to assist in organizing a 'Friends of Pierce Mill' association or committee to plan a fund-raising effort."[8] Abbott received dozens of telephone calls, and within three months, the organization was formed, giving hope that Peirce Mill's wheel would turn for a third century.

NOTES

Abbreviations

ES   *The Evening Star* (Washington, D.C.)

NI   *National Intelligencer* (Washington, D.C.)

WTH   *Washington Times-Herald*

WP   *The Washington Post*

HL   Records of Fitz Water Wheel Company, Hagley Museum and Library, Wilmington, DE

KRL   Kiplinger Research Library, The Historical Society of Washington, D.C.

LOC   Library of Congress

MRCE   National Park Service Museum Resource Center, Landover, MD

NAB   National Archives Building, Washington, D.C.

NACP   National Archives, College Park, MD

NPS   Records of the National Park Service

RG   Record Group

SC   Swarthmore College Library

CHAPTER ONE

1   Frederick Tilp, *This Was Potomac River* (Alexandria, VA: n.p., 1978), 328. George Washington, of course, was convinced the Potomac River was the key to an expansion of trade with the western territories that would boost the new country's economy to unprecedented heights. Washington also had a strong interest in the Potomac location for the new capital because of his canal-building enterprise along the river and his ownership of land on the Virginia side of the federal district. See Fergus M. Bordewich, *Washington: The Making of the American Capital* (New York: Amistad, 2008), 53–65.

2   Frederick Gutheim, *The Potomac* (Baltimore: Johns Hopkins University Press, 1986), 104.

3   Accounts differ as to when Jonathan Shoemaker first took up residence in Washington. For his purchase of the mill, see District of Columbia Deed Liber K10, Folios 117, 118, RG 351, NAB.

4   Friends of Peirce Mill and Quinn Evans Architects, *Peirce Mill Historic Structures Report* (Washington, D.C.: n.p., 2000), Appendix 1 (hereafter *Peirce Mill HSR*).

5   Frederick B. Tolles, *Meeting House and Counting House: The Quaker Merchants of Colonial Philadelphia* (Chapel Hill: University of North Carolina Press, 1948), 53.

6   Rosemary S. Warden, "Chester County," in John B. Frantz and William Pancak, eds., *Beyond Philadelphia: The American Revolution in the Pennsylvania Hinterland* (University Park: Pennsylvania State University Press, 1998), 1–19.

7   Sydney E. Ahlstrom, *A Religious History of the American People* (New Haven: Yale University Press, 2004), 265–66.

8   Thomas Lynch Montgomery, ed., *Pennsylvania Archives,* 5th ser., vol. 5 (Harrisburg, PA: Harrisburg Publishing Company, 1906), 820.

9   Gilbert Cope, *Genealogy of the Baily Family* (Lancaster, PA: Wickersham Publishing, 1912), 59.

10   Ibid., 35.

11   See entries under search results for "Abner Cloud" on the Virginia Land Office page at: http://ajax.lva.lib.va.us; "Offer of sale of land by Abner Cloud and Jesse Bailey," *Centinel of Liberty and Georgetown Advertiser,* July 22, 1796 (available at LOC); "Articles of Agreement between Richard Arell and Abner Cloud, Oct. 29th, 1783," "Agreement with Philip Doddridge about the 5,000 acre tracts," Feb. 21, 1827 (the latter two are copies, in possession of the author, of original documents whose whereabouts are unknown. The copies were provided by the Colonial Dames chapter that maintains the Abner Cloud House in Washington, D.C.).

12   Commissioners of Public Buildings to Isaac Peirce, May 6, 1799, vol. 5, 239, *Commissioners of Public Buildings, Index to Letters Sent, 1791–1839,* RG 42, NAB; "Agreement, Advance, and Accounts Allowed with Isaac Peirce," *Commissioners of Public Buildings, Index to Proceedings, 1791–1802,* RG 42, NAB.

13   The Maryland General Assembly, which had authority over the future area of the District of Columbia until 1800, passed an act in 1799 approving the road. William Kilty, *Laws of Maryland,* vol. 2 (Annapolis, MD: Frederick Green, 1800), November 1798, chap. 77.

14   For an authoritative history of the canal, see Robert J. Kapsch, *The Potomac Canal: George Washington and the Waterway to the West* (Morgantown: West Virginia University Press, 2007). For a report on the Little Falls section of the canal, see Dan Guzy, "The Potomac Company's Canal and Lock at Little Falls," *Maryland Historical Magazine* 96 (2001): 421–39.

15 *NI*, July 19, 1802; *Washington Federalist*, April 13, 1802 (available at LOC); *Record of Inventories*, Register of Wills Office, Washington County, 1807–1815, 271–72, 303, RG 21, NAB. For further insights into the Cloud family and the mill site, see: *Archeological Excavation of the Abner Cloud House* (West Chester, PA: National Heritage Corporation, 1976); George J. Olszewski and Charles S. Pope, Abner Cloud House Historic Structures Report (Washington, D.C.: National Park Service, United States Department of the Interior, 1966).

16 Mary E. Lazenby, "'Footing It' on Maddox Branch," undated article from the *American Motorist* magazine, in possession of author.

17 *Federal Republican*, February 5, 1813 (available at LOC): Probate files, estate of Abner Cloud Jr., Old Series Administration Case File 531, RG 21, NAB. Interestingly, these extensive probate files make no mention of Cloud's mill or income from the operation. William E. Davies, a U.S. Geological Survey official, wrote a short paper (undated, in possession of the author) about the mills near Little Falls, based on court and land records, in which he discusses the Clouds' acquisitions along the canal, the 1792 court decision on use of the canal's surplus water, and the sale of the Cloud mill. More research could reveal further details about the mill during the first years of the nineteenth century. Davies speculated that it operated under various owners up until the 1889 Potomac River flood that put the canal out of commission for two years and deprived the mill of its water supply.

18 *NI*, September 22, 1813.

19 Jonathan Shoemaker paid the "effective supply tax," a supplemental levy to help finance the military effort. His brother, David Shoemaker Sr. (1755–1825), is listed as a member of the sixth company, sixth battalion of the militia. *Pennsylvania Archives*, 3rd ser., vol. 15 (Harrisburg, PA: Harrisburg Publishing Company, 1906), 388; *Pennsylvania Archives*, 6th ser., vol. 1, 909.

20 Jay Worrall Jr., *The Friendly Virginians: America's First Quakers* (Athens, GA: Iberian Publishing, 1994), 275.

21 Edwin Morris Betts, ed., *Thomas Jefferson's Farm Book* (Princeton: Princeton University Press, 1953), 366–76.

22 Edward Shoemaker, *Some Account of the Life and Family of George Shoemaker* (Washington, D.C.: n.p. 1881), 3.

23 Worrall, *The Friendly Virginians*, 275. Ellicott was one of the founders of the Potomac port of Occoquan, Virginia.

CHAPTER TWO

1   James Sterling Young, *The Washington Community 1800–1828* (New York: Harcourt, Brace & World, 1966), 22–23.

2   *NI,* May 17, 1802 and January 5, 1803.

3   The original 1805 scroll signed by Jefferson, Peirce, and others is in the collection of the Washingtoniana Division of the Martin Luther King Public Library in the District of Columbia. For background on the establishment of the Lancaster School in Washington, see Harry Oram Hine, "Public Education in the District of Columbia, 1805–1928," in *Washington Past and Present,* vol. 1, ed. John Clagett Proctor (New York: Lewis Historical Publishing, 1930).

4   *NI,* January 9, 1812.

5   Richard Henry Spencer, ed., *Genealogical and Memorial Encyclopedia of the State of Maryland* (New York: Higginson, 1919), 251–55.

6   District of Columbia Deed Liber AS, Folio 391, RG 351, NAB.

7   *The Courier* (Washington, D.C.), May 27, 1812 (available at LOC).

8   *NI,* December 19, 1814.

9   District of Columbia Deed Liber AN, Folio 114, RG 351, NAB.

10 Quoted in John McPhee, *The Founding Fish* (New York: Farrar, Straus and Giroux, 2002), 163.

11 William Bushong, *Rock Creek Park Historic Resource Study* (Washington, D.C.: National Park Service, United States Department of the Interior, 1990), 27.

12 Charles H. McCormick, *Milling in Rock Creek Park* (Washington, D.C.: National Park Service, United States Department of the Interior, 1967), 15.

13 Tench Coxe, *Arts and Manufactures of the United States of America, for the Year 1810* (Philadelphia: n.p., 1814), as cited by Robert Lundegard, "Country and City Mills in Early American Flour Manufacture and Export," unpublished 2007 draft manuscript in possession of the author.

14 McCormick, *Milling in Rock Creek Park,* 6.

15 Bushong, *Rock Creek Park,* 27–28.

16 *Peirce Mill HSR,* 1.1.2.; Eugene S. Ferguson, *Oliver Evans: Inventive Genius of the American Industrial Revolution* (Greenville, DE: The Hagley Museum, 1980), 10–11; 52–53.

17 *Peirce Mill HSR,* Appendix 2: 1–7.

CHAPTER THREE

1   Elizabeth A. Hanson, "The Woodville Collection: Five Generations in Georgetown," *Washington History* 11 (1999), 66–67.

2   *NI,* October 26, 1840 and April 12, 1841.

3   Hanson, "The Woodville Collection," 66–69. Putting the family expertise and connections to use, George's son David L. Shoemaker formed his own firm, D. L. Shoemaker & Co., which ran two mills nearby. The first, known as the Foundry Mill (a former cannon manufacturing site), stood on the north shore of the Potomac on the western edge of Georgetown. It produced "Evermay" brand flour, which according to a contemporary account was popular as far away as New York and Boston. The Foundry Mill's daily capacity was 120 barrels of flour, along with 200 barrels of cornmeal. After the Civil War, D. L. Shoemaker & Co. bought the old mill of Abner Cloud, which since his death had passed through a number of hands. There, the firm produced another 120 barrels daily of Evermay. Cloud's wife, Susanna Pimmett Cloud, and her second husband continued to live at the canal house until 1852. *ES,* September 21, 1869, Olszewski and Pope, *Abner Cloud House,* 4.

4   David Shoemaker Sr. is listed as a member of the Sixth Battalion of the Philadelphia County Militia. See Chapter One, note 17. For details on his postal service position and the General Post Office, see *A Register of Officers and Agents, Civil, Military, and Naval, in the Service of the United States* (Washington, D.C.: Davis & Force, 1822), 1; Wesley E. Rich, *The History of the United States Post Office to the Year 1829* (Lawrence, MA: Quarterman Publications, 1977), 182.

5   *NI,* May 19, 1814 and July 23rd, 1825.

6   Reflecting on Shoemaker's drowning, Adams, who was nearly sixty, wrote that he seriously considered ending his daily swim in the river, but then concluded it was "in this climate indispensable [*sic*] to my health," and that, in any event, "we . . . must be in the hands of God." John Quincy Adams's diary entry for July 22, 1825, at http://www.masshist.org/jqadiaries/.

7   Family lore has David Shoemaker Jr. serving as an officer in the U.S. Navy during the War of 1812, but that was in fact his first cousin, Georgetown resident David Potts Shoemaker, brother of flour inspector George Shoemaker. See Edward Callahan, ed., *List of Officers of the Navy of the United States and of the Marine Corps from 1775 to 1900* (New York: Haskell House Publishers, 1969), 496. David Shoemaker Jr. was a private in the Washington, D.C., militia. See: War of 1812 Pension Application Files, National

Archives Microfilm Publication M313, roll 84, NAB. Pierce Shoemaker, unlike most others in his extended family, sometimes spelled his name this way ("ie"), as did his son, Louis Pierce Shoemaker. This led to the use of this spelling for the mill during most of the twentieth century. As "Peirce" is the dominant family spelling, it was adopted in the 1990s as the current name for the mill.

8   *NI*, May 25, 1820.

9   Louis P. Shoemaker, "Historic Rock Creek," *Records of the Columbia Historic Society* 12 (1909), 44. Louis Shoemaker kept many records, including what he said were English patents for the family land dated 1734. Most of these records have been lost, making it almost impossible to reconstruct the details of the two-thousand-acre claim.

10   Last Will and Testament, Isaac Peirce, November 14, 1835. Old Series Administration Case Files, Book 5, 240–43, RG 21, NAB.

11   These details came out in a D.C. court case *(Ould vs. Peirce)* concerning Isaac Peirce's bequests. See depositions of Jacob Holye, Horatio Lank, and Henry Chamberlin, in D.C. Chancery Case File 0215, RG 21, NAB.

12   *NI,* October 20, 1848.

CHAPTER FOUR

1   The earliest colonists in the mid-Atlantic territories had been struck by the profusion of native grapevines. Adlum wished to make an American wine "superior to the best cider as a wholesome beverage and equal to most imported wines." Upon tasting some of Adlum's early efforts, Thomas Jefferson pronounced them "very fine," comparable to a French red Burgundy. "I think it would be very well to push the culture of that grape without losing our time and effort to search of foreign vines which it will take centuries to adapt to our soil and climate," Jefferson wrote to Adlum. *Sunday Star,* July 29, 1917.

2   Shoemaker, "Historic Rock Creek," 46; *The Magazine of Horticulture, Botany, and all Useful Discoveries and Improvements in Useful Affairs* 8 (1842), 173.

3   Shoemaker, "Historic Rock Creek," 45.

4   David Warden, *A Chorographical and Statistical Description of the District of Columbia* (Paris, France: Smith, 1816), 58–59.

5   Peirce's city property was bordered by what would become Q, U, Fourteenth, and Sixteenth Streets, NW. Improvements on the land were never assessed at more than

$250, so it appears that besides a rustic farmhouse Peirce did not build a substantial structure or storefront on Fourteenth Street, which he gave as the address of his nursery. The assessment of the land rose steadily through the 1840s and 1850s, and by 1859 was set at more than $50,000. See illustration of Peirce farmhouse by Delancey Gill (drawing No. 32), in *Becoming the Capital City: Delancey Gill's Washington* (Washington, D.C.: The Historical Society of Washington, D.C., 1992); *Tax Books, Corporation of Washington,* 1850 and 1855; *General Assessments, Corporation of Washington,* 1844 and 1859, RG 21, NAB.

6   *NI,* June 21, 1833, August 1, 1833, August 29, 1833, June 8, 1836, and December 5, 1839.

7   "With The Rambler," *Sunday Star,* April 16, 1916.

8   *The Columbian Muse,* inscribed with Joshua Peirce's name on the title page, is in the collection of the Georgetown University Library.

9   Perry Wheelock, *Linnaean Hill Cultural Landscapes Inventory* (Washington, D.C.: National Park Service, United States Department of the Interior, 2003), Part 2a, 7–8; NI, June 30, 1841.

10   See 1857 Catalog for Linnaean Hill, Special Collections, National Agricultural Library, Beltsville, Maryland; *ES,* Oct. 22, 1856.

11   Entry for July 1, 1848, Proceedings of the Levy Court, Washington County, 1848–1857, RG 351, NAB.

12   *NI,* May 2, 1845.

CHAPTER FIVE

1   Jean Soderlund, *Quakers and Slavery: A Divided Spirit* (Princeton: Princeton University Press, 1985), 148.

2   A recent paper by a National Park Service intern notes that one of the two individuals, George Dover, is classified as "mulatto" on the emancipation petition of Peirce Shoemaker, "which in the District of Columbia means of racially mixed parentage. This description suggests a variety of possibilities about the Dover family structure." The assessment of George Dover's mixed parentage may also then apply to another man enslaved by the Peirces, James Dover, the intern observed, "since it is assumed they were brothers. Due to the frequency of sexual abuse inflicted upon black women during slavery, it is likely that the father could have been white and the mother could have been a black enslaved person of Isaac Peirce. This possibility could leave one to wonder

if Isaac Peirce could have fathered these children. If so, it would explain why these were the only two enslaved children indicated in the Bible of Isaac Peirce and why their names were just as ornately inscribed as those of his own white children." Izola T. Shaw, "The Link Revealed: A History of the Peirces' Enslaved Population," unpublished manuscript, 2003, 6, in possession of the author.

3   Isaac and Joshua Peirce were not among the signers. U.S. Congress. Senate. Document 191, "Memorial of a Number of Citizens of the District of Columbia," 25th Cong., 3rd sess., February 7, 1839, 1–4.

4   *NI,* January 25 and March 4, 1839. *Washington Federalist,* June 17, 1809 (available at LOC).

5   *NI,* October 28, 1842.

6   D.C. District Court, October 1854 term, Civil Trials File 238, RG 21, NAB; Minutes of U.S. Circuit Court, November 13, 1854, M1021, NAB; Dorothy S. Provine, *District of Columbia Free Negro Registers 1821–1861* (Bowie, MD: Heritage Books, 1996), 347, 483.

7   *NI,* November 2, 1842.

8   *Sermons by Thomas Wetherald, Delivered in the Friends Meeting, Washington City, March 20 and 27, 1825* (Philadelphia: n.p., 1825), 31–32.

9   The granddaughter was Elizabeth Cloud Peirce (daughter of Job Peirce), who married Henry Ould, uncle of Robert Ould Jr. Georgetown, in fact, was the center of a large pro-Confederate community; Allen Tate's 1938 novel, *The Fathers,* masterfully captures the mood of this period in its portrayal of a Virginia family and its links across the Potomac.

10   Tanya Edwards Beauchamp, "Mount Pleasant Historic District" (Washington, D.C.: D.C. Historic Preservation Office, 2000).

11   Dorothy S. Provine, *Compensated Emancipation in the District of Columbia: Petitions under the Act of April 16, 1862* (Westminster, MD: Willow Bend Books, 2005).

12   Benjamin F. Cooling, *Jubal Early's Raid on Washington 1864* (Baltimore: Nautical and Aviation Publishing Company of America, 1989), 129–53.

13   Edgar Turner to John Fitz, January 9, 1935, *HL.*

14   U.S. Census, Washington D.C., 1850.

18 *Shoemaker, "Historic Rock Creek,"* 41, 45, 47.

19 Ruth Butler to Verne Chatelain, February 21, 1935, Peirce Mill restoration workshop
    binder, in possession of the author. Apparently, the mill was used for social events
    even before the end of its commercial life in the 1890s. An "elderly dame" interviewed
    by a reporter in 1903 recalled a picnic and dance at the mill: "When the great big full
    moon came up that night all the boys and all the girls fell in love and many tender
    words were said and vows pledged only to be broken that beautiful September night."
    The Washington Times, December 13, 1903.

20 *ES,* Nov. 25, 1916.

21 Barry Mackintosh, *Rock Creek Park: An Administrative History* (Washington, D.C.:
    National Park Service, United States Department of the Interior, 1985), 18–39.

22 Bushong, *Rock Creek Park,* 113.

23 Horace W. Peaslee to C. S. Ridley, November 22, 1919, Rock Creek File, Commission of
    Fine Arts Records, RG 66, NAB.

24 Clarence O. Sherrill to Warren J. Brown, Dec. 19, 1921, General Correspondence File,
    Buildings and Grounds Records, RG 42, NAB, as cited in Mackintosh, *Rock Creek Park,* 31.

CHAPTER NINE

1 Ruth Butler to Verne Chatelain, February 21, 1935.

2 Allen C. Clark, "The Old Mills," *Records of the Columbia Historical Society* 31–32, 81–115.

3 For a comprehensive account of the origins of the historic preservation movement,
   see William J. Murtagh, *Keeping Time: The History and Theory of Preservation in America*
   (New York: John Wiley & Sons, 1997), 25–38, 51–61.

4 T. H. Watkins, *Righteous Pilgrim: The Life and Times of Harold L. Ickes 1874–1952*
   (New York: Henry Holt, 1990), 550.

5 Fay Campbell Kaynor, "Thomas Tileston Waterman: Student of American Colonial
   Architecture" *Winterthur Portfolio* 20 (1985): 103–32.

6 *ES,* June 14, 1967; Ruth Butler to Verne Chatelain, November 20, 1934, NPS,
   Correspondence and Reports Relating to Surveys of Historic Sites and Buildings,
   1934–1964, District of Columbia Reports File, 1934–1937, RG 79, NACP.

7 Bushong, *Rock Creek Park,* 137.

8 Neil M. Clark, "There'll Always Be Water Wheels," *The Saturday Evening Post,*
   December 3, 1955.

9 Thomas T. Waterman to Thomas C. Vint, July 7, 1936, Peirce Mill restoration workshop binder; *WTH,* November 19, 1936.

10 John S. Fitz to Marshall Finnan, October 11 and 22, 1935, December 31, 1935; Fitz to Fred Hinman, February 24, 1936, Box 457, HL.

11 *WP,* January 11, 1937, May 20, 1938.

12 Poem by Walter Hough, dated October 22, 1935, NPS, RG 79, NACP.

13 *WTH,* February 26, 1936.

14 United Press, "Ickes Puts $19,200 in Old Mill With Nothing to Grind but Ifs," February 26, 1936, NPS, District of Columbia Reports File, 1934–1937, RG 79, NACP.

15 "PWA Project 571," article dated July–August 1935, Peirce Mill restoration workshop binder; Fitz to Charles Peterson, May 5, 1935, Thomas Gray to Fitz, September 19, 1936, box 457, HL.

16 Gable to Tolson et al., June 26, 1936, NPS, District of Columbia Reports File, 1934–1937, RG 79, NACP.

17 A. E. Demaray to Harold Ickes, January 14, 1937, NPS, District of Columbia Reports File, 1934–1937, RG 79, NACP.

18 Ickes to Demaray, January 17, 1937, NPS, District of Columbia Reports File, 1934–1937, RG 79, NACP.

19 Barry Mackintosh, "Interpretation in the National Park Service: A Historical Perspective," at http://www.nps.gov/history/history/online_books/mackintosh2/index.htm.

CHAPTER TEN

1 "Justification for Construction of a New Dam at Peirce Mill," July 12, 1940, Peirce Mill restoration workshop binder; Associate Director to Ickes, March 30, 1942; Ickes to Prentiss M. Brown, March 12, 1943, Box 2834, NPS, Central Classified Files, 1933–1949, National Capital Parks, RG 79, NACP.

2 *ES,* January 24, 1943.

3 Mackintosh, *Rock Creek Park,* 106

4 *WP,* September 15, 1970; *Baltimore Sun Magazine,* March 3, 1957; invoice, Fitz company to Department of Interior, November 30, 1944, Box 457, HL. Background on Watt and Wolf: Ted Hazen, e-mail messages to author, July 2008. Hazen discovered that Watt had worked as a miller's helper at the St. Vincent College grist mill in Latrobe, Pennsylvania.

5   *WP*, August 17, 1964.

6   *WTH*, February 3, 1940.

7   Eric Sloane, "The Mills of Early America," *American Heritage* 6 (1955), 104.

8   SPOOM was chartered in Maine in 1972. See: www.spoom.org.

9   Murtagh, *Keeping Time*, 64–66.

10 *ES*, September 9, 1965; *Peirce Mill HSR*, 1.2.9; Fitz to Preston Riddel, February 9, 1965, Box 457, Records of Fitz Water Wheel Company, HL; *WP*, August 17, 1964.

11 Blaine Cliver, an architect working for the Park Service, wrote a report in the period recommending that the overshot wheel replace the breast wheel, and that a longer headrace be constructed. Closely examining detailed nineteenth-century maps, he said excavations should be used to find the original trenching, and that the new headrace be reconstructed along that alignment. Cliver also suggested placing large rocks in Rock Creek to divert more water into the headrace, and demolishing the concrete and boulder decorative dam (next to the mill) built in 1904. See "Historic Structures Report, Part 1," February 1967, Box 11, Rock Creek Park Files, MCRE.

12 "No written documentation can be found to explain exactly why these (1960s-era) decisions were made," according to the NPS unattributed draft document, "Environmental Assessment: Peirce Mill," March 3, 1978 (located in Peirce Mill restoration workshop binder). Though the reasoning is fairly obvious—it was the easiest thing to do—the decisions seem to contradict a general movement in historic preservation toward more authenticity, not less.

13 C. R. Currie to J. A. Martinek, December 21, 1969. Box 11, Rock Creek Park Files, MRCE.

14 *WP*, September 15, 1970, January 8, 1973; Robert Batte memo, June 22, 1979, Box 11, Rock Creek Park Files, MRCE.

15 Ogden quoted in Patricia O. LaLand, "The Legacy of Water Mills," *Early American Life* 22 (2001): 46.

16 Ogden, "Specification for Proposed Conversion of Water Source at Pierce Mill from City Water to Creek Water," October 1977. Paper in possession of the author.

CHAPTER ELEVEN

1   All Ted Hazen quotes in this chapter are from author interviews and e-mail exchanges, between November 2007 and July 2008, or from Hazen's autobiographical web page: http://www.angelfire.com/folk/molinologist/experiences.html.

2   "Crafts of Early America Series," Rock Creek Park brochure, summer 1987, Box 11, Rock Creek Park Files, MRCE.

3   http://www.angelfire.com/journal/millrestoration/interpretation.html.

4   Richard Steacy to Julia Washburn, January 3, 1997, Box 11, Rock Creek Park Files, MRCE.

5   A Delaware millwright who inspected the mill in 1987 warned that while "current staff has done quite well with what they have to work with," the entire mechanical system is "historically questionable, basically worn out, and cannot work right because of design problems." "Peirce Mill Condition Report 1987" (Greenville, DE: The Howard Company, 1987). Unpublished report in possession of the author.

6   Ogden, "Report of Findings at Peirce Mill, Rock Creek Park," 1997. Unpublished report in possession of the author.

7   Gray to Fitz, October 12, 1936, Box 457, HL.

8   *WP*, September 29, 1996.